Ivermectin for the World

"If you take it, you will not get sick."
- Dr. Pierre Kory, FLCCC

"May we please start saving lives now?"
- Dr. Tess Lawrie, WHO Consultant

Justus R. Hope, M.D.

Copyright © 2021 by Justus R. Hope, M.D.

All rights reserved.

Published by Hope Pressworks International, LLC, Redding, California.

Printed in the United States of America. No part of this book may be used or reproduced in any manner whatsoever, whether electronic or mechanical or stored in a data base or retrieval system, without written permission except in the case of brief quotations embodied in critical articles and reviews. For information, address Hope Pressworks International LLC, 5000 Bechelli Lane, Suite 102, Redding, California, 96002-3553

Second Edition

Library of Congress Cataloging-in-Publication Data has been applied for.

ISBN: 978-1-7374159-0-9

Cover by Daniel Ojedokun

DISCLAIMER

The information presented in this book is the result of years of practice, experience, and clinical research by the author. However, it is not a substitute for evaluation and treatment by a medical doctor. The information contained herein is for educational purposes only. It is not intended to be a substitute for professional medical advice. The reader should always consult with his or her physician to determine the appropriateness of the information for his or her own medical situation and treatment plan. No prescription medication should be obtained or taken without a personal physician's prescription, care, and supervision. Reading this book does not constitute a physician-patient relationship. The stories in this book are true. The names and circumstances of the stories have been changed at times to preserve privacy.

By Congressman John Lewis
1940-2020

Co-Organizer of the 1963 March on Washington
Co-Leader of the 1965 March on Selma
Presidential Medal of Freedom Award
Robert F. Kennedy Book Award
John F. Kennedy Profile in Courage Award

"When you see something that isn't right – isn't fair, that isn't just – you have a moral obligation to say something, to do something."

***

By Albert Schweitzer, MD, PhD
1875-1965

Priest, Physician, Humanitarian and Concert Musician
Medical Missionary
Founder of the Schweitzer Hospital of Lambaréné, Gabon
Goethe Prize Award
Nobel Peace Prize 1952

"The purpose of human life is to serve and to show compassion and the will to help others."

CONTENTS

Introduction 5

Chapter 1 10
Repurposed Drugs For Covid-19 10

Chapter 2 17
The Early Brave Pioneers Of Repurposed Covid Drugs 17

Chapter 3 53
Misrepresentation Of The November Senate Hearings: "The Fix Is In" 53

Chapter 4 75
The Second Senate Hearing: Enter Dr. Pierre Kory 75

Chapter 5 98
From Across The Pond: Dr. Andrew Hill Joins The Fray And The Nih Reacts 98

Chapter 6 126
Ivermectin Goes To Court 126

Chapter 7 157
Court Battles Give Rise To David V. Goliath Showdown 157

Frequently Asked Questions 194
Afterword 202
Epilogue: India's Natural Experiment 210
Post-Script: Cancer & Viruses 245
About The Author 253

INTRODUCTION

T he message of this book is simple. India is in an unprecedented humanitarian COVID-19 crisis at this time, and a solution exists.

As a practicing physician, this book is my way to contribute, and it is my great honor to present you with this powerful and positive life-saving information. The book is both inspirational and sobering at the same time, so please do not feel depressed as the very next chapter will be uplifting, I promise. Stay the course and finish the book, and you will be glad you did.

It is too late for vaccines to stem the tide of deaths immediately, and now India's cases are spiraling out of control. The last two days saw record and exponential increases in cases rising to 345,000 while deaths rose to 2,800.

While the vaccines have shown some protection against the original SARS-CoV-2 strain, they have proven far less effective against the mutant versions which seem to plague

Introduction

India today. These strains spread more easily, and they may prove to be more lethal if these numbers continue.

In contrast to vaccines, Ivermectin works immediately in all stages of the disease, and often a single dose can liberate a patient off the ventilator. It is effective as an antiviral agent against all variant strains. It is safer than Tylenol and most over-the-counter vitamins, and it costs only pennies per dose.

While this information may be the opposite of what you have heard in the news, I ask that you at least read the book before you decide that I am wrong. This book is currently offered free as a Kindle ebook, so there should be no issue with anyone being unable to afford it. It is short and filled with photographs, so it is an easy and compelling afternoon read.

If nothing else, please at least have a look at all the pictures and graphs. They are convincing, and most people can see that in a five-minute review. Leaf through the pages.

All I ask in return is that you fairly weigh the evidence. If you are a Christian like me, you will want to share this with your pastor or minister. If you are of a different faith, you will want to share it with your Rabbi or Priest. If you are atheist or agnostic, you may wish to act on moral or ethical grounds to support my message.

The bottom line is that the distinguished scientists and researchers I discuss all believe that the simple and effective Nobel Prize-winning antiparasitic drug Ivermectin can reduce death by up to 80 to 90 % in even the most advanced COVID-19 patients. It can transform a breathless, dying patient within hours into someone who can easily breathe on their own. Moreover, it can prevent almost everyone from ever getting infected. God, Himself could not have designed a much better drug for use in this pandemic.

As a physician with nearly 40 years of experience, all my patients have the option of Ivermectin. They have all done well with no deaths.

Ivermectin worked within 48 hours in each infected case.

But please read the evidence from the academic physicians with far superior credentials to mine. Please read about the legal cases where the hospitals fought against multiple dying patients on ventilators. When the court ordered the Ivermectin, they recovered in every one of these cases. Many were able to go off the ventilator with a single dose.

Read about why the news stories you have heard from the so-called "top doctors" in America may have been tainted and may have twisted the science against you. I am not an antivaxxer. I recommend the vaccines. However, I also recommend Ivermectin because the vaccines miss some variants, particularly the South African Strain.

Finally, I review the Senate Testimony of the true experts, not the talking heads you see on television that speak but never actually treat, I review the testimony of those doctors who practice in the trenches. Those doctors who save almost all of their COVID-19 patients, those doctors who care more about saving lives than accumulating money.

The message of this book is to first enjoy the stories in this book, and the second is to follow your heart to save lives in India. Please pardon my drama; however, the truth is that Indian people are dying in front of hospitals while gasping in taxi cabs. They are waiting in line for hours to enter the hospital. These Indian citizens have children and

Introduction

spouses like you and me. They love their family just as much as you and I.

However, they do not have the same access to quality medical care. They feel breathless like you or I when we cannot breathe. They suffer, and they die. Their loved ones grieve.

In the pages that follow, allow me to give you a refreshing glimpse of physicians in action and the science of how doctors can save almost everyone from COVID-19. How you can make a difference by helping those in India breathe again, get back to health again, and escape death.

Allow me to paint pictures of inspiration and success and tell you true stories of patients celebrating their recovery with their doctors, stories of Dr. Fareed and Dr. Tyson, and The Miracle of the Imperial Valley.

Allow me to show and tell, through photos and poetry, of just how these doctors worked their miracles and why Pandemics don't always have to be about the doom, gloom, and fear we all see on the evening news.

This book contains a refreshing and uplifting anthology of slices of time during the pandemic, served up in chronologic order, including stories about physicians like Dr. Albert Schweitzer, Dr. George Fareed, and Dr. Pierre Kory.

But at the conclusion of the book, I will ask you to help us save lives. We do not want money. We need your help in the form of a call to action to spread the word. My fellow physicians and I cannot do this alone. We are being censored and ridiculed. We are being vilified. Merely speaking out places us at risk.

8

Ivermectin for the World

However, you do not have a medical license and are immune. You can do what many physicians cannot. You, as a concerned citizen, can speak out. You can protest. You can ask your pastor or Rabbi to tell the congregation. Facebook, YouTube, and the powers that be cannot stop your message as they can suppress ours.

Please read this book, and act. Even if your act is small, like sharing this book with merely two other people, that simple act can save lives now in India.

I invite you to join me, Dr. Lawrie, Dr. Kory, Dr. Fareed, Dr. Risch, and Dr. McCullough in this noble movement to save India with Ivermectin.

Chapter 1

REPURPOSED DRUGS FOR COVID-19

What exactly is a repurposed drug?

Great question.

The simple answer is that a repurposed drug means using of any FDA-approved drug for an off-label purpose. Off-label use means prescribing a medication for another purpose other than its approved one. For example, pediatricians use antibiotics off-label some 20% of the time.

Tricyclic antidepressants are used every day for chronic pain, antipsychotics are used for dementia, and anti-seizure medications are used to treat fibromyalgia. Without off-label use, millions of patients could not receive adequate treatment. Colchicine, an effective gout treatment, was used 50 years before any FDA approval or testing was done. Without the off-label use of this drug, millions would have suffered for decades.

Off-label use allows doctors to help patients with conditions that have not gone through billions of dollars of Phase I, Phase II, and Phase III FDA testing, as well as jumping through regulatory and political hoops to get FDA approval.

"Many people may be surprised to know that the FDA regulates drug approval, not drug prescribing, and ... doctors are free to prescribe a drug for any [reason they think is medically appropriate]," says G. Caleb Alexander, MD, MS, a medical ethics advocate and assistant professor of medicine at the University of Chicago Medical Center. "Off-label use is so common, that virtually every drug is used off-label in some circumstances."

So, when it comes to terminal cancer, let's say, where someone will likely be dead in one year with the standard approved treatment of chemotherapy, radiation, and surgery, off-label use prescribed by your doctor, can in some cases save your life.

An excellent example is that of Dr. Gregory Riggins and his mice. When his mice with brain cancer got pinworms, he treated them with mebendazole, an approved pinworm drug. The mice were cured of pinworms and miraculously also their cancers.

Soon the cancer-treating properties of mebendazole surfaced and many began taking the pinworm treatment for their own cancers.

Such bypassing the FDA is legal as Dr. Alexander has pointed out. However, let us mention that it is frowned upon by oncologists and leading government-funded scientists.

They don't much care when a pediatrician treats an ear infection with an off-label antibiotic. No one loses any money over that. But when you start treating terminal cancer off-label, eyebrows will be raised.

If cancer treatment with repurposed drugs raises eyebrows, the mere suggestion of off-label use of drugs to treat coronavirus causes heart-stopping political debates, and indeed exactly the types of ad hominem attacks you have witnessed all over the news about that dirty word:

Hydroxychloroquine.

Hydroxychloroquine, once the darling of Lupus and Rheumatoid Arthritis patients for decades, mysteriously became a violent killer overnight. However, just as mysteriously, the FDA has not banned its use for Lupus, and no attorneys are advertising class action lawsuits against it. It only becomes dangerous - and unprofitable for some - if you wished to use it off-label for COVID.

Hmmm.

If you or a loved one have cancer, you will want to learn all you can about The Repurposed Drug Revolution.

If you or a loved one are worried about Coronavirus, this is the most important book you may ever read.

Questions & Answers about Repurposed Drugs

Q: Why would the FDA, CDC, WHO, NHS and other agencies that are charged to protect our health be against repurposed drugs if they could save us from cancer or COVID-19. You would think that they would be the first to publicize and promote them if they truly were effective, correct?

A: No

Q: What are repurposed drugs?

A: Drugs FDA-approved for one purpose that are prescribed off-label for another.

Q: Are there any repurposed drugs for COVID?

A: Depends on who you talk to. FDA says no. Most docs say yes.

Q: What are examples of repurposed drugs?

A. Anti-depressants are used every day to treat chronic pain. Antibiotics are used every day by pediatricians to treat ear infections. Antipsychotics are used to treat dementia.

Q: Why is the FDA against the use of repurposed drugs?

A: The official reason is that without FDA approval, the drugs either may not work, or they may be dangerous. The unofficial reason is that billions of dollars in testing: Phase I, Phase II, and Phase III trials are required to get that stamp of approval. And there is money to be made by many players, including Big Pharma, the FDA, the NIH, and the middlemen.

Q: What is the greatest argument by physicians for the use of repurposed drugs without FDA approval.

A: Doctors are trained to use all drugs scientifically based upon their judgment even without FDA approval. More than 20% of all drugs are used off-label without FDA approval in cancer, for infections, and when FDA-approved drugs do not exist, as in the coronavirus.

Repurposing Drugs for COVID-19

Q: What are examples of non-FDA approved drugs that can help?

A: Dr. Riggins found that his mice with brain tumors, when treated for pinworms, with a deworming drug, mysteriously got cured of their brain cancers. Riggins began researching Mebendazole, the pinworm drug and found that it had powerful anti-cancer effects by blocking microtubule formation in cancer cells. Soon doctors began prescribing this drug for patients with terminal cancer, with positive results much to the dismay of the FDA.

Q: What are examples of repurposed drugs for use against the coronavirus?

A: Kaletra, an HIV drug made up of Lopinavir/Ritonavir, has shown potent effects against the first coronavirus, SARS CoV-1. It has also shown positive results against the novel coronavirus, SARS CoV-2. Other repurposed drugs have been used effectively in other countries: Camostat, Favipiravir, and Hydroxychloroquine. Most recently, Ivermectin has shown the most powerful and consistent benefits when used to prevent and treat COVID-19. Throughout all stages of the disease, the data from over 50 studies has shown Ivermectin to demonstrate consistent and substantial reductions in death.

Q: Why is the FDA against the use of these drugs?

A: The official answer is that the studies do not support their use. The unofficial reason is that repurposed drugs make little money. They are off-patent, meaning they can make very little money. They were branded to make money off their original purposed. Now they are cheap and generic, and anyone can make them. The FDA much prefers drugs like Remdesivir as it is not repurposed. It has not been FDA approved for general widespread use for anything before, so it can and will be patented and is expensive.

Q: Can repurposed drugs be life-saving?

A: Absolutely.

Q: What must I know about repurposed drugs?

A: Repurposed drugs historically have been opposed whenever they have been found to be effective. They are unprofitable because they are no longer on patent. As an example, the drug Wellbutrin XL oral tablet, extended release carries a cost of $ 1,665.16 according to drugs.com.
This would be the patented version's price for thirty tablets or a one-month supply. The generic version of the drug, the off-patent price for bupropion oral extended release for thirty tablets averages just $ 34.75 for a one-month supply.

In this case, the generic drug is 98% cheaper than the branded or patented version. This is the reason repurposed drugs will never be approved so long as pharmaceutical companies enjoy a cozy relationship with the agencies that regulate them and have the power to approve these drugs.

Q: If Ivermectin is already proven so effective, why not just use it around the world in the billions of doses right now and end the Pandemic?

A: Ivermectin does not make anyone real money as it costs only pennies to make: 100 pills can be made for around $ 2.40, and it can be purchased in the Dominican Republic for 83 cents a pill. Any pharmaceutical manufacturer can produce it in bulk by the millions of tablets in less than one week.

But the real problem is this: According to Dr. Pierre Kory of the FLCCC Alliance, any admission that Ivermectin works could harm the vaccine effort, and therein lies the rub. The vaccine investment is far too large to endanger. Currently the vaccines are approved only as "Emergency Use Authorization" meaning no effective alternative exists. If Ivermectin were shown effective and approved as standard therapy for COVID, "that would kneecap the entire global vaccine policy around the world" in the words of Dr. Pierre Kory.

The vaccine industry is already counting their profits to be had in the coming years. An announcement was recently made that a third "booster" vaccine shot may be necessary in six months. And this may be followed by annual COVID (compulsory) vaccinations. Multiply this by a few billion people each go around, and you may begin to see precisely why the world is being misled.

Chapter 2

THE EARLY BRAVE PIONEERS OF REPURPOSED COVID DRUGS

Shortly after the pandemic began, in late February or early March of 2020, many doctors began to improvise. Repurposing existing drugs was logical, and as I also discovered, Hydroxychloroquine (HCQ), seemed like the best candidate. Thus, I scoured the available data on HCQ's effectiveness against SARS-CoV-1, the close relative to SARS-CoV-2. And HCQ had a dramatic effect, at least in the lab, against it.

Dr. Fareed, a former virologist at the NIH, and acclaimed AIDS pioneer, now working in the small town of Brawley, also read the same studies. In France, Dr. Didier Raoult, a giant in the virology world, also read these. Didier went a step further and did the first human trials, much to the dismay of Big Pharma and the FDA.

The Early Brave Pioneers of Repurposed COVID Drugs

When Raoult's preliminary data suggested that COVID-19 could be stopped with HCQ, a cheap and repurposed drug costing pennies, the powers that be had to stop it. They discredited Raoult first, writing smear pieces in the New York Magazine. They ridiculed his long hair, accused him of mistreating his staff, and attacked his eccentric behavior. They took advantage of Donald Trump's support of the drug. Let us begin our journey into repurposed COVID drugs with Dr. George Fareed who became an icon in the pandemic.

Dr. George Fareed

Dr. George Fareed uses Repurposed Drugs to treat COVID-19 with great success. He is a country physician practicing in the Imperial Valley of Southern California, and has enjoyed remarkable success with the use of a repurposed drug cocktail combat the pandemic - and he and his colleagues have treated thousands with no ill effects - despite the media and the official positions against Hydroxychloroquine (HCQ).

Dr. Fareed is not your ordinary country doctor.

He was named the CMA Rural Physician of the Year in 2015. He is now in his seventies. But early in his career he served as professor at both Harvard and UCLA Medical Schools.

He used repurposed drug cocktails to treat AIDS patients during that epidemic. Dr. Fareed knows a thing or two when it comes to treating viruses, and he does not agree that HCQ is too dangerous to employ when used carefully.

Dr. Fareed wrote a letter to the White House Task Force and to Dr. Anthony Fauci. In this letter he agreed that HCQ is not useful in the advanced stages of COVID-19; however he believes the scientific studies support a role early in the outpatient phase when it can save lives. He states:

> *The HCQ cocktail can be used for outpatients to prevent hospitalizations and thus keep our hospitals and ICUs from being overrun with COVID patients.*
>
> *The HCQ cocktail can be used early on in hospitalization to prevent patients from requiring mechanical ventilation and reducing the length of hospital stay.*
>
> *HCQ/zinc can be used for prophylaxis for high risk individuals including front line health providers, first responders, and even teachers who are at high risk for COVID.*

Today, we know that while HCQ may be safe and effective for early treatment of COVID-19, we also know that Ivermectin works both early and late in the disease. It can save lives by its dual antiviral and anti-inflammatory mechanisms of action. Dr. Fareed today has modified his protocol and treats his outpatients with both HCQ and Ivermectin.

We know that Ivermectin is effective in ventilator patients as well as outpatients. We know it can effectively prevent the disease. And we are now accumulating evidence that it works in the long-hauler's COVID syndrome as well.

Everyone needs to know about repurposed drug cocktails. They work for more than just terminal cancer. Scientists have now shown with more than 50 studies including dozens of randomized and controlled that Ivermectin can save hundreds of thousands of pandemic lives now.

For the sake of humanity, for the sanctity of human life, and for our inviolable right to medical care, we must use it in India immediately as they face a horrid second pandemic wave now in the springtide of 2021.

DR. GEORGE FAREED & THE MIRACLE OF THE IMPERIAL VALLEY

Dr. George Fareed knew about a treatment for COVID-19 that was covered up. A treatment so effective, so scientific and so simple, that he had to share it with his community and his country. It was his duty; his ethical obligation as a physician.

Dr. Fareed had such values instilled at an early age by his father, himself a medical pioneer. The senior Dr. Fareed had worked with Dr. Albert Schweitzer and been influenced by his core values. In 2020 it was time for Harvard-trained cancer researcher Dr. George Fareed to muster the courage to stand up against perhaps the most powerful opponent in any medical fight, the head of the NIAH, the leader of the CDC and FDA, Dr. Anthony Fauci himself.

Dr. Fareed was up to the challenge, and he did not back down. George is a man of quiet but powerful expression. His words have moved mountains. Already his actions have influenced a community of physicians in the Imperial Valley of California to treat their citizens with his life-saving triple therapy, a treatment inspired by the work of Dr. Didier Raoult and Dr. Vladimir Zelenko.

This treatment has resulted in the saving of countless lives locally. However, Dr. Fareed was not satisfied in just saving the Imperial Valley. He knew that the nation needed to hear the message, so he wrote an "Open Letter to Dr. Anthony Fauci" to call the nation's leading spokesman for healthcare policy to task on his colossal failure to recognize this valuable treatment.

The Early Brave Pioneers of Repurposed COVID Drugs

There is no easy way to say it. Dr. Fauci's policies have [in Dr. Harvey Risch's words]
"led to the deaths of hundreds of thousands of Americans who could have been saved by usage of this drug." Dr. Fareed has been threatened by the Medical Board. He has faced his share of criticism. However, Dr. Fareed's reputation is beyond reproach. He holds patents on cancer drugs. He has worked at the NIH as a cancer and virus researcher. He has taught at both Harvard and UCLA schools of medicine.

Now in his seventies, Dr. Fareed aims to get the word out that this Pandemic can be stopped in its tracks tomorrow if only everyone learned the truth. If only Dr. Fauci were called to answer the questions posed in Dr. Fareed's letter.

This letter was originally published in his local newspaper, The Desert Review. That was published online, and is how I learned about Dr. Fareed and the Miracle in the Imperial Valley.

That letter has since been republished in my book, *Surviving Cancer, COVID-19, and Disease: The Repurposed Drug Revolution*. It has been my great honor to get to know this gentle medical giant of a man. Dr. Fareed's letter has launched a Congressional Inquiry by Rep. Louie Gohmert and Sen. Rand Paul.

He has appeared on the Sean Hannity Program twice. Soon, as millions of people find out about him, I have no doubt he will get an audience with Dr. Anthony Fauci. Soon his questions posed in the "Open Letter" will have answers.

In the words of Dr. Albert Schweitzer,

"Truth has no special time of its own. Its hour is now - always."

HARVEY RISCH, MD, PHD

Dr. Harvey Risch calls for the immediate, widespread and early use of Hydroxychloroquine to treat the early stages of COVID-19. He writes that we have already lost tens of thousands of lives because of not using it, and we could lose even more if we do not start as soon as possible.

He is not a fringe doctor.

In fact, he is the Associate Editor of The Journal of the National Cancer Institute. He is an Epidemiologist of world renown.

Harvey Risch, MD, PhD
Professor of Epidemiology (Chronic Diseases)

The Yale Website describes him as follows:

Dr. Harvey Risch is Professor of Epidemiology in the Department of Epidemiology and Public Health at the Yale School of Public Health and Yale School of Medicine. Dr. Risch received his MD degree from the University of California San Diego and PhD from the University of Chicago.

After serving as a postdoctoral fellow in epidemiology at the University of Washington, Dr. Risch was a faculty member in epidemiology and biostatistics at the University of Toronto before coming to Yale.

Dr. Risch's research interests are in the areas of cancer etiology, prevention and early diagnosis, and in epidemiologic methods. He is especially interested in the effects of reproductive factors, diet, genetic predisposition, histopathologic factors, occupational / environmental / medication exposures, infection and immune functioning in cancer etiology.

His major research projects have included studies of ovarian cancer, pancreas cancer, lung cancer, bladder cancer, esophageal and stomach cancer, and of cancers related to usage of oral contraceptives and non-contraceptive estrogens.

Dr. Risch is Associate Editor of the *Journal of the National Cancer Institute*, Editor of the *International Journal of Cancer*, and Member of the Board of Editors, the *American Journal of Epidemiology*.

Dr. Risch is an author of more than 325 original research publications in the medical literature, has an h-index of 88, and is a Member of the Connecticut Academy of Sciences and Engineering.

When it comes to the subject of the use of HCQ for COVID-19, do you believe anyone that advises against it on CNN, The Nightly News or the Task Force? Those who speak but never treat?

Or maybe someone like Dr. Harvey Risch ?

Dr. Albert Schweitzer

Dr. Albert Schweitzer won the Nobel Peace Prize in 1952. Chloroquine has been studied extensively in the Albert Schweitzer African Hospital in Gabon.

"The purpose of human life is to serve and to show compassion and the will to help others."
-Albert Schweitzer M.D.

Allow me to answer the reader's questions about HCQ and CQ (chloroquine). I researched both extensively in my quest to find a repurposed drug that could help my patients while a vaccine was being developed.

Q: Does Chloroquine cure COVID-19?

A: No.

Q: Does Chloroquine help in the advanced stages, during the Cytokine Storm?

A: No.

Q: Is Chloroquine potentially dangerous?

A: Yes. It carries cardiac and eye toxicity at high doses and when used for long time periods.

Q: Is Hydroxychloroquine or HCQ safer than Chloroquine?

A: Yes. Much safer.

Q: Can HCQ cure COVID-19?

A: The recent data look promising if the drug is used early in the disease before the Cytokine
Storm has set in.

Q: What is the recent data?

A: The Henry Ford study, published in July, 2020, looked at 2,500 patients. Those who were prescribed HCQ early, within the first two days of hospitalization, were compared to a control group that did not receive the drug. The two groups were followed. When the study was completed, the HCQ group had a 13 % death rate compared to the no-HCQ group who suffered a 26% mortality.

The HCQ was associated with decreasing the death rate by half.

The recent study published by Sholtz, Derwand, and Zelenko implemented the HCQ even earlier, within 3 to 4 days of symptoms, BEFORE HOSPITALIZATION.

The group that received HCQ enjoyed 80% less chance of hospitalization and 84% lower risk of death.

The Chatterjee Study in India looked at PROPHYLAXIS, the use of HCQ preventatively. 400 mg of HCQ was given once weekly to front-line health care workers. They were compared to health care workers who did not receive the drug.

After six weeks and six doses, those health care who received HCQ enjoyed an 80% reduction in the risk of contracting COVID-19.

Q: But isn't it true that the top experts all advise against the use of HCQ?

A: Define "Top Expert." If this is someone who speaks but does not treat, someone whose advice changes by the day, then yes, I have heard him as well. But if you mean the editor of The International Journal of Cancer, the famous Dr. Harvey Rich, MD, PhD, of the Yale School of Public Health, he agrees with the above.

If you mean "top expert" in the sense of Harvard-trained Dr. George Fareed, who was awarded the presitgious Plessner Award by the California Medical Association making him the 2015 Rural Physician of the Year, the same Dr. George Fareed who Pioneered the AIDS Clinic in the Imperial Valley of California, whose father worked with Dr. Albert Schweitzer, and the same physician who has treated over 1,000 COVID-19 patients with HCQ, and not had one death, then yes, Dr. Fareed also agrees with the answers in this review.

Q: So, what you are saying is that the top Harvard and Yale doctors who actually treat patients, the true experts, are interpreting the studies as showing effectiveness of HCQ against COVID-19?

A: Let me answer it this way. Allow me to quote Dr. Harvey Risch. Don't take my word for it. Read what Dr. Risch wrote in Newsweek on July 23, 2020:

"Since publication of my May 27th article, seven more studies have demonstrated similar benefit. In a lengthy follow-up letter, also published by AJE, I discuss these seven studies and renew my call for the immediate early use of hydroxychloroquine in high-risk patients.

These seven studies include: an additional 400 high-risk patients treated by Dr. Vladimir Zelenko, with zero deaths; four studies totaling almost 500 high-risk patients treated in nursing homes and clinics across the U.S., with no deaths; a controlled trial of more than 700 high-risk patients in Brazil, with significantly reduced risk of hospitalization and two deaths among 334 patients treated with hydroxychloroquine; and another study of 398 matched patients in France, also with significantly reduced hospitalization risk. Since my letter was published, even more doctors have reported to me their completely successful use."

Q: So are you saying everything about what we have heard in the media, the claims that HCQ is bad for you, that it will harm your heart, that it doesn't work is false? Are you saying the media has lied to us?

A: That's not the issue. The issue is not the mistakes we have made in the past. It is what we can do and should do now in moving forward. We are in a position to save hundreds of thousands of lives going forward.

The answer was put most eloquently by Dr. Harvey Risch:

"For the sake of high-risk patients, for the sake of our parents and grandparents, for the sake of the unemployed, for our economy and for our polity, especially those disproportionally affected, we must start treating immediately."

DR. HARVEY RISCH CALLS OUT PANDEMIC CORRUPTION

Dr. Harvey Risch recently gave a revealing interview on the COVEXIT.com forum on October 24th, 2020. The interviewer was Oxford-trained Jean-Pierre Kiekens. In this interview, Dr. Risch commented on the wealth of evidence for effective repurposed drug use against COVID-19, the best way to treat high-risk nursing home patients, and why the FDA and CDC have not gotten behind these treatments.

Along these lines, allow me to briefly first report on an email received today from a Mississippi physician, Dr. J.B: He reports his personal experience with COVID-19:

> *"May I relate my personal experience with Covid? A month or so ago, I noticed during Friday afternoon clinic I was having to run to the bathroom to urinate after every patient. Unheard of for me. Urinalysis was normal except concentrated. After work, I was febrile and had the nurses test me for Covid with our Sofia 2. Positive. Repeat, positive. I had it. Went to bed with low grade fever.*

Saturday, I was sicker than ever before in my life with a high fever.

I experienced Godawful arthralgias and myalgias, dyspnea, and a headache that could only be described as explosive. I wrote my wife a list of instructions in case I became incapacitated and went to bed wondering if I would survive the night. Sunday morning, imagine my delight to find that, not only had I survived, I was completely well! Monday, I retested (twice) and both results were negative.

The secret? I had started myself on everything I thought might improve my chances within 2 hours of symptom onset. They were zinc, nebulized budesonide, Eliquis (coagulopathy prophylaxis) and hydroxychloroquine based on the Ford Foundation study that showed unequivocally a 50% reduction in mortality with HCQ. Clearly, this would be classified as "anecdotal" but I'm convinced this combination cured me. 74 year-old patients just don't get one-day episodes of Covid."

In an email today he further stated: "My nurse's recovery was more dramatic."

But my hands are tied in terms of prescribing HCQ because the Mississippi Medical Board has specifically not endorsed its use and I could be sued in the case of an adverse event.

It is beyond me that results like those cited in the Ford study can be completely ignored and even suppressed. I find myself wondering if, beyond the obvious political implications, there are corporate sponsors of expensive hospital treatments like Regeneron, whose therapies would be rendered instantly irrelevant if the word got out, which are involved in the coverup." Signed --Dr. J.B. Mississippi

Dr. Risch spoke of the convincing evidence for HCQ/ZINC/Azithromycin provided by many including the data from Dr. Zelenko, Dr. Proctor, and Dr. Tyson. He noted that most drugs are approved without the benefit of randomized controlled trials. He noted the double standard used in the Pandemic due to the excuse (ruse) of needing double-blinded randomized controlled studies first. When asked why the governmental agencies did not approve these treatments in the face of now overwhelming evidence they work, Dr. Risch did not hesitate:

"There has been a lot (of what I'll call) malfeasance in this Pandemic about how to treat it. The financial interests are so large, they've corrupted the playing field. That's what's behind the great amount of reliance of non-scientific reasoning and the corruption of bureaucracies and governments. The 200,000+ Americans who have died, have lost their lives because of this corruption."

Watch Dr. Risch's interview on COVEXIT.

https://youtu.be/cf3_YXR70Ug

DR. BRIAN TYSON, ALL VALLEY URGENT CARE PHYSICIAN IN EL CENTRO, CALIFORNIA

Dr. Bryon Tyson is an associate of Dr. Fareed. Dr. Tyson owns and operates All Valley Urgent Care in El Centro, California. El Centro is a border town located about 20 miles south of Brawley. Dr. Brian Tyson has already saved thousands of lives. He took out a 250,000 dollar loan personally to order Personal Protective Devices and COVID-19 testing equipment when he could not acquire these from the Health Department or CDC.

Dr. Tyson is a no-nonsense doctor who practices in the trenches of COVID-19. He treats migrant farmworkers and meat-packing house employees who don't have the luxury of social distancing. Dr. Tyson is a warrior.

He has now treated 1700 patients with COVID-19 and saved every single one of them. Not a single death. Only one hospitalization.

Did he make medical history or win a Nobel Prize? Or did he receive the Presidential Medal of Freedom Award?

No.

He was informed that his license might be in jeopardy if he were to treat more patients with HCQ. This drug has acquired a bad name through fraudulent and retracted studies, a drug that has been safely used for decades. This drug has only recently been demonized by political opponents of the President.

Watch Dr. Tyson's Interview where he explains all of this. And read the book, *Surviving Cancer, COVID-19 and Disease: The Repurposed Drug Revolution*. If you are worried about COVID-19, turn off the television, turn off CNN, save the *New York Times* for wrapping fish, and get the truth from Dr. Tyson.

Who says they don't censor in America?

https://youtu.be/fe1TqxvXKTs

Doctors rarely use terms like miracle. It is considered unscientific by some. I suppose other doctors might be worried about criticism. However, during the COVID-19 Pandemic when the FDA and CDC tell you that there is no effective prevention or treatment for COVID-19 and a physician documents almost 2,000 cases in a row of cure, the word "miracle" comes to mind.Dr. Tyson's story is the stuff of legend.

It is tantamount to a miracle when the U.S. and world economies have been brought to their knees from the Pandemic. When the so-called top experts in the United States have reported that the only hope in sight is a vaccine that must be rushed.

Today, in 2020, the American public is asked to believe that cowering at home in fear behind masks is the "new normal" and that to do anything else is both unscientific and unpatriotic. I might have believed this too, had it not been for the fortuitous occurrence of brain cancer in one of my colleagues: a health care professional I had known for 30 years.

I had to do everything possible to help him, including questioning the status quo and standard treatment of chemo/radiation/surgery. I researched the world medical literature. And I found that repurposed drug cocktails could offer better survival chances. This was in accord with known studies and accepted science. However, it was not supported by the "old guard", those groups affiliated with Big Pharma and Big Tech.

The old boys club wanted patients to submit to the standard treatment that typically costed $100,000 and resulted in death. I grew angry. I realized that I had never been taught about the benefits of repurposed drug cocktails. I told my friend and his family. He has received them - some of these drugs against the advice of his oncologist. However, his tumor is shrinking. He is defying the odds, and ten months into this, he is improving.

This led to repurposed drugs for COVID-19. Now Dr. Tyson has treated 1900 patients with COVID-19 with the same repurposed triple-drug cocktail to which my readings also pointed. And every patient was cured. Guess what? This cocktail is prohibited in almost 40 states by the "old guard." The time has come for repurposed drug cocktails to be used to save lives, whether they are politically correct or not.

All Americans are guaranteed the right to "Life, Liberty and the Pursuit of Happiness" regardless of the profit motive of corrupt governmental agencies. That is why I wrote and published the book *Surviving Cancer COVID-19 and Disease: The Repurposed Drug Revolution.* In this book, you can learn about these drug combinations that can save your life from everything from AIDS to Terminal Cancer to COVID-19.

And you can read about Dr. Tyson's First Person Account of COVID-19, first published in the book. Read about the story that motivated cancer expert Dr. George Fareed to take on Dr. Anthony Fauci and launch a Congressional Inquiry. Learn about the most remarkable scandal and coverup in history since Watergate. Learn about the health care fraud that has caused the needless deaths of over 200,000 Americans.

Read the story of "The Miracle of the Imperial Valley." You will never look at health care again the same.

THE MIRACLE OF THE IMPERIAL VALLEY [1]
Dr. Tyson's First-Person Account of COVID-19

Originally published in Surviving Cancer COVID-19 & Disease, The Repurposed Drug Revolution

The Start

We heard about a virus coming out of Wuhan, China, in January of 2020. I had a feeling it was going to make its way to the US due to all the international travel. I told my wife Fabiola; we need to get prepared, and we are going to need a plan. It was long before we started hearing of cases across the US; Washington had the first outbreak and then New York. I remember getting a call from my daughter Mahkenna's music manager Gary Salzman, who she was supposed to fly out and see in late March for her new single.

Gary told me, "I think I have this crap!"

I replied, "How do you feel. Is it bad?"

He said, "It's in my lungs, and I'm having a hard time breathing."

I suggested he go to the ER and get tested to be sure and get available treatment. I had done some research from studies coming out of southern France by Dr. Didier Raoult. A study published by the *Journal of Virology* in 2005 showed Chloroquine was a potent inhibitor of SARS Coronavirus Infection and spread.[2]   I told him to get on Hydroxychloroquine, Zinc, and Z-pack.

His response was that he was just at the ER, and they sent him home with no treatment and said he was not even sick enough to test him. Without that ability to test, treatment as an outpatient was withheld. It wasn't until he became sicker and later ended up in the hospital that they paid any attention to him.

Gary died two weeks later. We were devastated as a family; the music community lost a legend, and we could not even have a funeral. I told myself that I would not allow that to happen with any of my patients. I would find a way to test people and treat people when that day comes.

March

It's now March, and we see the virus all around us. We are scared. My staff was scared, my wife was scared, my parents and In-laws are scared. We have young staff members with newborn kids, others with small kids, and we have small kids and a teenager with Down's syndrome. We had no idea how our lives were about to change.

It's mid-March, and we are seeing sick patients, but we have no tests. We have a screening tool sent out by public health that was not helpful at all to try to determine if patients may or may not have COVID 19. Upper respiratory infections are common in March. What's the difference between COVID 19 symptoms and Influenza? Travel? We are a border town. Many people live in the town of Mexicali (population 1.5M) and work in the Valley (190K).

We are now screening patients outside with a pop-up tent, tables, and some chairs. MAs are scared but strong and take vitals and history from everyone in their cars. They report back to me, and we see them outside in their chairs once the registration process is done. We still had no way to test. I called the hospitals, Public Health, and the Abbott representative to see if we could get the ID kits now that the FDA had approved them because we have the machine already, and the answer was "no" across the board.

There was no way to find out who was positive and who needed treatment. We were now frustrated and scared at the same time. My wife said we should close until we can figure it all out. I was not going to give up. I called all my contacts, and out of the blue, my good friend Terrance found a Lab in Orange County, Equitox, that could get me the serology tests that would show if your IgM or IgG immunity was present.

At last, we had a tool. We also started doing Chest X-rays on all patients with respiratory symptoms. It was not long before we were able to identify the COVID 19 pattern on Chest X-ray and using the IgM, IgG approach. We started treatment on patients. We began with Hydroxychloroquine 400mg by mouth twice a day on the first day, then 200mg three times a day for days 2-5. We would re-evaluate everyone in 2-3 days and see them back at 7 and 14 days to make sure they did better. We also wanted to confirm immunity for patients who then needed to go back to work.

April

By the end of March and April, we were now seeing 200-400 patients a day. We were asked by many essential workers to help keep their services and businesses open. We took care of the many local establishments: the Border Patrol, Calipatria and Centinela Corrections Officers, Homeland Security, Customs, Sheriff's Department, Brawley Beef, RoGar Manufacturing, Imperial Valley Auto, ICOE, and Imperial Valley Superior Court. We also saw many cattle feed and farming seed companies and the various medical and dental offices that needed to stay open.

We knew our system was not perfect, but it was the only one we had. We revised the tents and tables into an insulated carport with mobile clinic functions implemented to have air conditioning for summer, copy machines, registration, air-flow and disinfection on a regular basis.

There was still no way to confirm patients with PCR testing due to a lack of supplies. We didn't even have PPE.

I was called by the Public Health office and asked to stop testing because we were creating too much work for them, and we could not confirm our patients' infections. When I asked where else we could send them for confirmation, I was told the ER. The problem with that was (as my friend Gary told me) they were not sick enough to be tested. I was told by the ER's they only had ten swabs per week from each hospital, and only those sent to the ICU were being tested.

I then got a letter from the ER Medical Director at El Centro Regional Medical Center instructing me to stop prescribing Hydroxychloroquine because it would prohibit the hospitals from getting it for those who needed it. I could not believe what I was hearing. For the first time in my life as a physician, I was being told to stop saving people's lives! My response was clear, "Give me an alternative, and I will use it; Until then, I will use whatever I have that has been shown to work. "

I have never understood the pushback on using treatments that were maybe controversial but showed promise over the ridiculous policy of "Home Quarantine for 14 days" without any treatment.

Who does that? Since when is any disease treated by quarantine alone?

We have drugs that work and we have vitamins and supplements that help; why not at least use those? Why confine others at home with known sick people? These are still questions that nobody in the public health department wants to answer. We went to the meetings at public health and asked about the PPE stockpile and were told once again that nothing was available.

During this time, my staff and I were out at the large businesses giving lectures on the virus, how to prevent transmission and that the treatment seemed to be working if they got sick. That seemed to set the standard for our community. Cleaning, social distancing, staying home when not working, and not going to work sick. Early evaluation if symptoms occurred and mandatory seven days off and retesting if the serology test was negative. Mandatory 14 days off if positive.

May

In May, we finally had two labs that were able to get us the PCR nasal swabs. That was good and bad. We were able to finally confirm cases, but the bad was the level of work it took to call all the patients and get the test results out and make the follow-up and treatment calls. I knew all along that the possibility of getting in trouble was there, so we had been keeping a spreadsheet with all the positive patients and the treatment plan and recovery plan. It worked out when we got a call from the State and CDC in June after months of being left alone. We found out that our center was the only place that kept that level of records, and we were chosen to be the Sentinel Site for California and CDC for the Imperial Valley. We were finally validated that everything we did was worth it.

September

We made the news in late September and October when we started publishing our data, and people realized that we had seen more COVID-19 patients face-to-face than probably anyone in the nation, and maybe even worldwide. We did that and have not recorded a single death for anyone that was placed on (our) treatment. We did have to call EMS on two patients that presented to our Urgent Care in respiratory failure and were sent to the hospital before we could start treatment. One of those died, and for the other, we were unable to get follow-up information. As of today, we have over 1900 COVID-19 positive recovered patients – a 100% success rate!

This brought the call to go to Washington, DC.

October

The process in preparation for speaking at the US Supreme Court was intimidating. Those invited were all highly intelligent physicians, scholars, lawyers, and researchers. I felt like I was out of my league. It was intimidating, and once again, I was scared. What will they think? What if I mess up? What if I get laughed at and ridiculed? I still needed to make a statement. I still needed to tell our story.

I still needed to be heard.

Dr. Simone Gold wanted a passionate speech with facts from all of us. After our meetings in DC and the recordings we all did, I felt it was my time. The fear had left me, just like it left me at the clinic in treating all the COVID-19 patients. The staff had been sick but survived. Students were sick and survived. Two of my Nurse Practitioners, both my sons and my manager's mom with MS, all got COVID-19 and survived. That is where my speech came from. It was the buildup and resolution of fear that had us all so scared in the beginning, but now realizing there is treatment.

My Speech

"We can go back to school! We can go back to work! We can go back to life! We can go back to being Americans! We will not let fear take our freedom!!!" I spoke on those steps.

That was a moment I will never forget. It truly was incredible. I have always wanted to do something great for my country, knowing that my grandfathers served in WW2, Vietnam, and Korea. I thought of my grandpa

Tyson. My dad served in Vietnam. How scared were they? What must it have been like to have to go into an actual war? This is my war, and it's not over.

We are still fighting the fight, and we will continue to do so. I hoped the video would be a tool that other physicians could see and hear. We need everyone to be able to see the success we had. When it was finally posted on YouTube, it was exciting, it started to go viral, and then something happened.

It was taken down!!

Why? Why would you take down a video with the knowledge, research, links, and website where everyone can see what we are doing! Why? I don't have any reason. I can't believe that Big Tech and Government controls want to see people die. Why would you take down the message of hope? Why would you take down the message of treatment? Why do you want to continue living in fear when there are clear treatment options now?

There are multiple options. Peter McCullough and his peers published the first peer-reviewed pathway to outpatient treatment in the *American Journal of Medicine,* and that too was recently taken down.[3] We had to get Senate influence to have them re-publish it!!

That should upset people all over the world.

Think about it, the world is looking to us to find a treatment or a cure, and when we do, it gets taken down? Most people would be like – WTF? I was able to channel that anger, I was able to get raw video, and we published it again and again.

We will keep publishing it over and over until it is recognized all over the world that we don't need to be afraid anymore. People need to know that we will survive this pandemic, just like those of the past. There is treatment available. It works when used early, and it is very effective.

We will get our voices heard because we hear the cry of those in our care. Physicians are people too; we have families and kids. We would never advocate for something we didn't believe.

Scientists are different; they have financial gains and incentives. They have research that needs to be funded, and while they may have the best of intentions, they do not work on the frontlines. They do not care for patients; they do not have to explain the risks and benefits of treatments. They are not there when patients break down and cry when they are told they have a positive test. They don't have to explain to a 9-year-old girl that she will not kill her parents just because she is positive.

Scientists have no skin in the game and no emotional pain when things don't go their way. This virus has killed people!! It will kill more. The question is, how many more will die unnecessarily due to not getting the available treatment?

How many will die in fear, and how many will die alone?

My final point is this: When you get sick, you do not go to the CDC or the NIH or call the FDA to get diagnosed and treated. You go to your doctor! You go to the people who have seen the disease before and know how to treat it. This virus is no different.

-Brian Tyson, MD
Board Certified in Family Medicine
14 Years of ER and Hospital Medicine Experience
All Valley Urgent Care in El Centro, California

References

1. Hope, J. *Surviving Cancer, COVID-19, and Disease: The Repurposed Drug Revolution.* Hope Pressworks International LLC. 2020 Redding, CA.

2. Vincent, M., Bergeron, E., Benjannet, S., et al. Chloroquine is a potent inhibitor of SARS coronavirus infection and spread. *Virol J.* 2005; 2:69.

3. McCullough PA, Kelly RJ, Ruocco G, et al. Pathophysiological Basis and Rationale for Early Outpatient Treatment of SARS-CoV-2 (COVID-19) Infection [published online ahead of print, 2020 Aug 7]. *Am J Med.* 2020;S0002-9343(20)30673-2. doi:10.1016/j.amjmed.2020.07.003

[Excerpted from the book, *Surviving Cancer, COVID-19, and Disease: The Repurposed Drug Revolution*]

Dr. Peter McCullough: Cardiologist & Repurposed Drug Visionary

Dr. Peter McCullough

Dr. Peter McCullough MD, MPH, has published over 1,000 peer-reviewed papers and is a respected Academic at the Baylor Heart and Vascular Institute.

He has advocated for early outpatient treatment of COVID-19 to decrease the likelihood of death and to stem the tide of the Pandemic. In a recent Webinar on the groundbreaking COVEXIT forum, he was interviewed by Jean-Pierre Kiekens.

During the interview, he covered the subject of his most recent of 20 peer-reviewed publications on early treatment of COVID-19.

He contrasted these recommendations with those of the country's NIH, which has no advice for early treatment other than social distancing, PPE and isolation.

Many other countries are more enlightened regarding the need for early treatment; Dr. Peter McCullough advises an algorithm approach that he recently published in August in the American Journal of Medicine. This calls for triple therapy in high-risk patients, including an antiviral, an antibiotic, and zinc. The antiviral can be either HCQ, Ivermectin, or Favipiravir.

Dr. McCullough dropped the bombshell that he, himself, had recently tested positive for COVID-19 and now was following his own advice. In a second surprise, Dr. Brian Tyson joined the webinar as a guest and announced that he was also recently diagnosed with the condition.
Both men will follow the triple therapy protocol.

Dr. Brian Tyson, also interviewed previously in COVEXIT, was the author of the stunning First-Person Account of COVID-19, first published in our newest title, Surviving Cancer, COVID-19 and Disease, and later published in COVEXIT and later the Economic Standard.

Dr. Tyson's Account is also entitled, "The Miracle of the Imperial Valley" as he treated 1900 patients positive for COVID-19 with ZERO deaths, an incredible verification of the effectiveness of Early Outpatient Treatment, and a vindication of HCQ. Dr. Tyson has single-handedly treated about 1/6 of Imperial Valley County's 12,500 cases of COVID-19. Statistics would have predicted that these 1900 cases would have contained some 50 to 60 deaths or 1/6 of Imperial Valley County's 350 deaths.

The fact he had no deaths speaks to the effectiveness of this treatment.

Dr. Peter McCullough, also an MPH and Epidemiologist, now joins the growing ranks of the outspoken critics of U.S. Health Care Policy in this Pandemic. Early effective treatment exists and has been shown both in the lab and in actual patient use to be safe and effective beyond any shadow of doubt.

Dr. McCullough is calling for the widespread use and acceptance of such early treatment. No reasonable scientist could disagree.

What do you say, Dr. Fauci?

Testifying for Repurposed Drugs

Originally published November 20, 2020

Today, November 19, 2021, three world-class medical experts testified in a Senate hearing about the best way to save hundreds of thousands of American lives over the next few months. They cited peer-reviewed publications, scientific evidence, observational evidence, and just plain logic. Dr. McCullough led the discussion by summarizing his peer-reviewed article advising early outpatient treatment for COVID-19.

These three physicians, considered icons in the medical world, used fact and arguments that can be found throughout the book *Surviving Cancer, COVID-19, and Disease: The Repurposed Drug Revolution*.

Senator Johnson summarized his feelings when he got sick:

"But I, as a patient myself, wanted to get Hydroxychloroquine, and I couldn't get it, ok? I think I should have the right to try, in dealing with my doctor, who I trust, I'm sorry, more than some of these people who are so outside the circle of empathy, and for whatever reason, I'm sorry, it's just me.

I question the fact that because this cocktail costs about $ 20, and Remdesivir costs $ 3,000, that maybe there's a little bias. Maybe there's a little conflict; maybe there's a little agenda outside of really what's treating a patient when you're in the ivory tower, and you're not dealing with sick and dying and ventilated patients."

This conflict of interest pervaded the difference between Dr. Jha's transparent arguments. He repeated the party line of "no good science shows HCQ to be effective" versus the volumes of data reported by Dr. Risch, Dr. Fareed, and Dr. McCullough, showing major reductions in death. Jha argued that the major medical and infectious disease societies and consensus favored the CDC's and FDA's position. Risch argued that science is not based on consensus.

Dr. McCullough and Dr. Risch spoke about the overwhelming evidence in support of early outpatient treatment with HCQ/Zinc/Azithromycin approaching 100% in some studies.

Dr. George Fareed asked the opposing expert, Dr. Jha, if he actually treated patients. Dr. Jha said he did, at the VA; however Senator Johnson clarified that Dr. Jha had never treated a single COVID-19 patient, yet was confident to say that "good science" did not support the use of HCQ.
Dr. McCullough countered that his studies were peer-reviewed and represented the best of science. He called Dr. Jha out and noted that he, Dr. McCullough, had published 20 peer-reviewed studies on the subject and Jha had not published a single one.

Dr. McCullough, a cardiologist at Baylor, and the Vice Chair of Internal Medicine, further pointed out that HCQ did not cause scarring to the heart, an argument that had been propounded by Jha's side, and that the Texas Heart Institute at Baylor was the premier such center in the world. Dr. McCullough went on to say that the CDC and FDA were guilty of scare-mongering and misinformation concerning the risks of HCQ.

He pointed out that academic fraud was further involved in the attempt to discredit repurposed drugs by HCQ and that this agenda went "far beyond republican versus democratic politics."

This has all been exhaustively detailed in the book: *Surviving Cancer, COVID-19, and Disease: The Repurposed Drug Revolution.*

Dr. McCullough warned,

"I don't hear a sense of urgency on this committee call at all. We are weeks away from mass panic and massive mortality. There are so many infected people now - we are hitting 20% positivity rates. And the average person infects many more people. This is a massive calamity that's right around the corner - and I'm asking and pleading for the Senate and America right now to not absolutely get clobbered with a Tsunami of mortality - particularly for our elderly citizens."

"This is a call for not just a small group of innovative doctors and researchers but for the broad medical community. We have a million doctors and half a million nurse practitioners sitting on the sidelines right now. Their patients are calling them, and they don't know what to do - the government is telling us to do nothing - and we don't treat COVID."

This is a call by all three doctors, and the author of this book, to use early outpatient treatment on all high-risk cases - and to start treating immediately - as Dr. Harvey Risch presciently wrote back in May of this year:

"It is our obligation not to stand by, just carefully watching as the old and infirm and inner-city of us are killed by this disease and our economy is destroyed by it, and we have nothing to offer except high-mortality hospital treatment. We have a solution, imperfect, to attempt to deal with the disease. We have to let physicians employing good clinical judgment use it and informed patients choose it."

https://www.c-span.org/person/?128373

Chapter 3

MISREPRESENTATION OF THE NOVEMBER SENATE HEARINGS: "THE FIX IS IN"

Dr. Raymond Chang is an Oncologist who trained at the Sloan-Kettering Cancer Institute and is considered one of the foremost authorities on Repurposed Drugs nationally and internationally.

He completed post-doctoral training at Yale and Cornell. He has taught at the Cornell School of Medicine and served as an attending physician at the New York-Presbyterian Hospital. He has written books and been interviewed on the Today Show and cited by Reuters, Fox News, ABC News, and WebMD, etc., for his pioneering work in using repurposed drugs in Oncology. He was featured in the ground-breaking documentary film "Surviving Terminal Cancer."

Misrepresentation of the Senate Hearings: The Fix is In

https://youtu.be/SV4epXiKgrM

Dr. Chang has candidly stated that cheap and repurposed drugs will "never" be approved because they threaten the profits of the richest pharmaceutical interests in our nation. Board members of these companies run deep into our government, and this inextricable link means the average citizen cannot expect honesty and integrity. When our former FDA chairmen sit on the boards of some of the wealthiest drug manufacturers in the world, we cannot expect industry and their brethren to choose our lives over their profits.

Corporations have a fiduciary duty to their shareholders to maximize profits, and this obligation supersedes the Hippocratic oath for many.

The purpose of this book is to bring the case for repurposed drugs directly to the people, as they are now in the best position to judge whether they should use them. We the people, now provided the true science, can exert the necessary pressure to insist on repurposed drugs. India is now in crisis. Now is the perfect time to call for massive deployment of Ivermectin. We must act to save hundreds of thousands of Indian people during this horrific second wave of COVID.

Here I now present articles written over the past half-year, articles that surround the slanting of life-saving Senate Hearing testimony: there is clear evidence of the demonization of any cheap, repurposed drug that shows effectiveness against COVID. I would emphasize that this tactic extends to repurposed drugs against terminal cancer, but that subject is covered in another book, *Surviving Cancer, COVID-19, and Disease: The Repurposed Drug Revolution.*

Ivermectin for the World

Prior to the Pandemic, Dr. Raymond Chang would have been correct in his assessment that repurposed drugs did not stand any chance of being approved because hundreds of millions of dollars would fund the media campaign to tarnish them and those who supported them.

However, now that their tactics have been laid bare by this pandemic and exposed in all their disgusting glory for the world to see, it is my sincere belief that repurposed drugs will enjoy a renaissance, and the floodgates will open. Repurposed drugs may now be used in India to end their Pandemic deaths, and they may be later used worldwide – not instead of – but in addition to – vaccines.

Once the truth becomes widely known, repurposed drug cocktails will be welcomed by most terminal cancer patients. Dr. Chang only dreamed of this before, but now it will become a reality as the majority of citizens come to learn about the corruption of our greatest scientific journals, institutions, and most storied medical leaders.

The following articles will lay bare the facts supporting this. It is no longer some vague conspiracy theory. It is true with dates, facts, and figures to support.

Misrepresentation of the Senate Hearings: What You Need to Know

This article was originally published November 23, 2020

Allow me to begin with a letter written by a physician who wishes to remain anonymous: (*I have deleted the name of his state and changed the name of the recipient and doctor to safeguard his privacy*)

Dr. Denver:

I am a family physician and have seen my patient population devastated by COVID-19 while I am constrained from providing early interventional care.

I am pleading with you and the board to watch the November 19 senate hearing convened by Senator Ron Johnson with three highly-esteemed physicians, Drs. Fareed, Risch and McCullough who have had dramatic, almost miraculous, success with a three-drug cocktail for early intervention and treatment of COVID-19. I have included a link below.

It is a tragedy that I and other of this state's physicians cannot prescribe these medicines without incurring legal and licensure issues.

These medicines have been in constant use for 65 years with no signs of significant side-effects. To proscribe their use in this particular limited case is inexplicable since off-label use of medicines is an established norm.

If these medicines were in widespread use, it is very likely that our hospital COVID-19 population would never have reached the level it did.

As you know, we are on the cusp of a pandemic crisis possibly unprecedented for many decades.

I ask you and the board to release our state's physicians from constraints in treating of this terrible disease.

In so doing, our state could provide guidance for the entire nation.

Sincerely,

Dr. Ryman

Dr. Ryman is referring to the Senate Committee Hearing of 11/19/20 where Dr. Harvey Rich, the esteemed editor of the International Journal of Cancer, Dr. Peter McCullough, the Vice Chair of Internal Medicine at Baylor, and Dr. George Fareed, the 2015 California Physician of the Year and former NIH researcher and Harvard Professor all testified before a Senate Committee chaired by the Honorable Ron Johnson of Wisconsin.

Dr. Fareed stated:

"I have a background in virology from a research standpoint from work at the NIAID (NIH) and as a Professor performing research at Harvard Medical School (after I graduated from Harvard Medical School in 1970 I became a professor there) and at UCLA School of Medicine. I have had 30 years of clinical experience, treating HIV and other infectious diseases as well as practicing primary care medicine."

Dr. Fareed went on to describe his experience in treating nearly 1,000 sick COVID-19 high risk patients with the triple therapy.

Misrepresentation of the Senate Hearings: The Fix is In

"The results are consistently good, often dramatic, with improvement within 48 hours. I have seen very few hospitalizations, and only a few deaths in patients that were sick to begin with and received the medication late while hospitalized.

I have not seen a single negative cardiac event and few other side effects, despite what we hear in the media. My experience is in-line with all the studies regarding early use of the HCQ cocktail.

Let me be clear, this is only about the science — the science of viral replication, the science of the stages of COVID, and the science why early treatment works."

These three exemplary physicians testified about the effectiveness of Early Outpatient Treatment of COVID-19 and referenced volumes of scientific and peer-reviewed studies while the opposing "expert", Dr. Ashisk Jha, did not. In fact, Dr. Jha did not even appear in person. He was the only expert that decided to testify by zoom. Dr. Jha admitted he had not treated a single COVID-19 patient. Dr. Jha admitted he had not authored a single scientific peer-reviewed paper on the subject. However Dr. Fareed had treated hundreds if not a thousand COVID-19 patients. Dr. McCullough has authored over 1,000 scientific peer reviewed papers with 20 on COVID-19.

These three experts trounced Dr. Jha, even made him look foolish.

Did the media fairly report this to you, the public?

No. The New York Magazine on November 20, 2020, commented negatively on Senator Johnson's sobriety in the first sentence. They described the hearing as a "headlong plunge into nuttery" and associated this all with Donald Trump. The esteemed writer, who is not a physician, referred to the three iconic physicians as the "few remaining oddball supporters of the drug (hydroxychloroquine)." This "journalist"went so far as to accuse Senator Johnson of promoting a conspiracy theory (because Johnson noticed the price of the FDA favored Remdesivir was 100x more than HCQ).

Who pays these people?

Who promotes this propaganda?

Let's talk about the issues; let's not make 8th grade personal attacks. Come on people! We have 250,000 deaths today and most of the these could have been prevented had we followed Dr. Harvey Risch's advice in May.

Now we are seeing on average 1500 American deaths per day, and no vaccine for most people until mid 2021.

That translates into another 250,000 deaths that can be blamed on Censorship and misinformation of the type I just cited above.

Not to mention that you will not hear about life-saving early treatment of the type these three testified about on YouTube. You will not see it on Amazon. I have written extensively about it.
And sadly, my colleague, Dr. Ryman, will get no positive response from his State Medical Board, because, as you might guess, it is also influenced by the regulators.

The bottom line is that if you want to be informed, please read my books. I don't pull any punches, and you will get the science and the truth.

Start with viewing the Senate Hearing for yourself: Judge for yourself the credibility of these three experts against the lone opponent. Don't bother to read the summary in the media. You already know what they will say. They will talk about the sobriety of the chairman, or Trump, or call them names like oddballs. But they will never discuss the real science.

https://www.c-span.org/person/?128373

"The Entire ...Biopharmaceutical Complex is Basically Corrupt" -Peter McCullough

Originally published November 26, 2020

These are the words contained in Dr. McCullough's sworn Senate testimony delivered last week.
https://youtu.be/ftq6lmRlKgQ

Dr. Peter McCullough pointed out that it is a "fool's errand" to test a single drug like Remdesivir late in the illness.

"This is no different than HIV. We need multiple drugs early up front (for COVID-19) and the best we have right now are these mixes of Vitamins, Supplements and generic medications."

"The NIH and the Biopharmaceuticals right now have delivered ZERO oral medications to doctors in practice. ZERO. That's our batting average right now. So as a country with the greatest phamaceuticals in the world, zero oral drugs for the next patient that gets COVID-19."

Ivermectin for the World

Why is Dr. McCullough so upset about not having oral drugs available in the US for COVID-19? Because oral medications allow "Early Home Treatment" which is life-saving with a virus.

Japan, Russia, and India ALL allow and use Favipiravir early, at home, and it is an oral version of Remdesivir. It is NOT allowed or available in the US.

Why? Certainly it is not because our technology is inferior to that of those other three countries. Look no further than to the title of this article for the answer.

Repeatedly Dr. McCullough pleads for the US Government to support the use of early outpatient treatment than has been through observational data nearly 100% effective in the series of thousands of cases reported by Dr. Brian Tyson, Dr. George Fareed, Dr. Vladimir Zelenko, and Dr. Proctor of Texas.

History will not look kindly on our government that turned a blind eye to these Senate recommendations if it turns out the Dr. Fareed, Dr. McCullough and Dr. Risch were correct. Who exactly will answer to the 250,000 deaths that science will later prove could have been saved if this treatment had been acknowledged and implemented?

On the other hand, assuming arguendo that Dr. Jha, the CDC expert is proved correct and these do not work, not one extra person will have died because the strategy was employed.

To summarize, if Dr. Peter McCullough proves correct and he is ignored, not only do we see 250,000 deaths today that could have been prevented, but all those additional deaths that are coming. We are at 2300 US deaths per day and rising. Assuming a vaccine is implemented to the majority of Americans by June, which is doubtful, we are looking at

6 months more of mortality: 180 days x 2300 deaths per day (assuming no increase) which amounts 414,000 MORE deaths.

Do we really wish to take the chance that if he is correct our regulators will have to explain why early treatment was not implemented, and why 664,000 Americans died in vain? If corruption is the reason, how will the country react?

I join Dr. Peter McCullough in his plea to awaken the country to get with the program, to make oral medications like Favipiravir available IMMEDIATELY to US physicians to prescribe with through Emergency Use Authorization AND to allow the other repurposed drug cocktails recommended by Dr. McCullough in his peer-reviewed article accepted and published in the American Journal of Medicine.

Reference: McCullough PA, Kelly RJ, Ruocco G, et al. Pathophysiological Basis and Rationale for Early Outpatient Treatment of SARS-CoV-2 (COVID-19) Infection [published online ahead of print, 2020 Aug 7]. *Am J Med.* 2020;S0002-9343(20)30673-2. doc: 10.1016/j.amjmed.2020.07.003

Censoring Dr. Tyson Part I

Originally published October 18, 2020

Censorship and Repurposed Drugs

That might be the title of my next book, provided I am not silenced. If I am, you will know who did it.

So, if the real title of our current book is *Surviving Cancer, COVID-19, and Disease: The Repurposed Drug Revolution*, why exactly am I writing about censorship? The answer is simple. The reason you probably have not heard about repurposed drugs for COVID-19 or Cancer is because of censorship.

Yesterday Dr. George Fareed's associate, Dr. Brian Tyson, traveled to Washington D.C. to be honored for his great service to the citizens of the Imperial Valley, a small county in the Southeastern portion of California, bordered by the Colorado River, the Salton Sea, and the Arizona California border as well as the California Mexico border.

Misrepresentation of the Senate Hearings: The Fix is In

This small desert community is known for its heat as well as its agriculture. It is also known as the COVID-19 epicenter of California. It contains small communities such as El Centro and Brawley. Dr. Tyson operates an Urgent Care Center which was inundated with COVID-19 cases. The Imperial Valley County has seen some 12,410 cases and 334 COVID-19 deaths.

Dr. Tyson treated 1900 of these cases with the triple therapy proven to be effective by multiple studies, and this resulted in zero deaths, one hospitalization and all with full recovery. There were no adverse effects.

All of the 334 patients who died from COVID-19 DID NOT RECEIVE his treatment.

Dr. George Fareed, an associate of Dr. Tyson is Harvard-trained, holds three patents on cancer drugs and was a researcher at the NIH before he became a "country doc" in Brawley. He has written an "Open Letter to Dr. Anthony Fauci" which is published in our book. Dr. Fareed is in good company with world scientists including the famed Dr. Harvey Risch of Yale who agreed with him and Dr. Tyson that the cocktail of HCQ/Zinc/Azithromycin is highly effective in preventing and treating COVID-19.

Dr. Tyson's results speak for themselves.

Dr. Fareed shared a video link of Dr. Tyson's speech with me. The speech was delivered in Washington D.C. yesterday on the steps of the U.S. Supreme Court. He eloquently relayed his clinical experience in saving countless lives in the Imperial Valley with this innovative and proven treatment.

Dr. Tyson's story along with Dr. Fareed's experience has been called, "The Miracle of the Imperial Valley" as science would have predicted that his 1900 COVID-19

infected patients treated with conventional therapy would have produced 3% mortality or some 54 deaths.
Yet Dr. Tyson saved at least 50 lives. Dr. Tyson's actions are a model for all physicians and should have been broadcast to patients and physician alike.

I posted his video speech and wrote about it on cancercovid.com

It was removed just a few hours later as part of a censorship effort. Apparently it violated "standards" on YouTube which include medical opinions held by non-medical YouTube personnel. Perhaps the real reason were opinions held by YouTube advertisers? Perhaps the most well-healed ones who sell expensive drugs that might compete with HCQ?

Fortunately books are not censored yet in America.

If you want to know what the Harvard and Yale trained experts are saying about the life-saving potential of Repurposed Drugs for both cancer and COVID-19, please read our latest book on The Repurposed Drug Revolution. You will not find the truth from the news, YouTube, Facebook or CNN. You will not hear the truth from our government-appointed health "experts" who unfortunately are involved in serious conflicts of interests with Pharmaceutical Corporations.

If you wish to find the truth, the way that expert physicians approach cancer for themselves or their loved ones, or how they approach COVID-19 for themselves or their loved ones, please read about The Repurposed Drug Revolution.

Censorship is alive and well in the United States when it comes to medical science.

Censoring Dr. Tyson Part II

Originally published November 28, 2020

The Imperial Valley

Why is it that Dr. Brian Tyson's story is so worthy of censorship?

As readers of my site may recall, the Imperial Valley of California recorded such a surge of COVID-19 cases in June 2020 that the National Guard was deployed. On June 13, 2020 the Desert Review reported,

"Imperial County recently experienced a surge in the number of COVID-19 positive cases that overwhelmed local hospitals, who in turn, sought assistance and resources from the State and Federal level."

El Centro Regional Medical Center CEO, Dr. Adolphe Edward stated, "It could be a combination between patients coming from Mexicali, Imperial County, and the opening of San Diego, and Yuma that contributed to the surge."

He continued, "If we keep the patients here, we will overwhelm the hospital." Edwards was desperate.

"We (will) transfer anywhere in California...I beg for my patients to be cared for," Edward said about patients transferred either by land or by air.

Dr. Brian Tyson and Dr. George Fareed, working at the local El Centro All Valley Urgent Care Center had a better solution. They improvised using the best science they had, and employed a technique that had proven successful in the hands of a New York Physician, Dr. Vladimir Zelenko. They treated patients early, usually within the first few days of the illness.

This was against the official CDC and FDA guidelines which called for no outpatient treatment; only sheltering in place and home quarantine.

Not surprisingly, Dr. Fareed's and Dr. Tyson's approach proved stunningly successful. They aggressively tested upwards of 20,000 patients, and some 1900 were COVID-19 positive. All 1900 were treated with the Zelenko protocol of triple therapy, a five-day course of Hydroxychloroquine, Zinc, and Azithromycin.

The proof was in the pudding. Not a single patient of theirs who was treated with the triple therapy died. Only one got sick enough to require hospitalization; and no one had to be transferred by land or air to another part of California. Dr. Brian Tyson and Dr. George Fareed had resolved the crisis in El Centro, and now their story is the stuff of legend. It is known as "The Miracle of the Imperial Valley" or alternatively as "Dr. Brian Tyson's First-Person Account of COVID-19."

Did Tyson or Fareed win a Nobel Prize? Were they invited to the White House? Did the California Health Department ask them to speak and share their life-saving protocol with the rest of the state's physicians?

No.

Dr. Tyson was asked to stop using Hydroxychloroquine.

He gave a press conference in Washington, DC, and offered a message of hope to the country, that effective treatment already exists, and that people no longer need to be afraid.

Was this message embraced and shared?

The YouTube video was taken down.

Dr. Tyson's incredible account was published as part of the book, "Surviving Cancer, COVID-19, and Disease: The Repurposed Drug Revolution."

Did it immediately rise to the top of the Best Seller Ranks? Did the world suddenly take note of how El Centro escaped a desperate situation where its hospital was being overwhelmed and the CEO was sounding the alarm requesting help from anyone and from anywhere?

The book suddenly was either "out-of-print" or "out-of-stock." Whereas prior to adding Tyson's Account, one could get it shipped within one to two days, after the story was added the book became "radioactive" and could not be shipped for one to two months.

In the UK, on Amazon, it remains listed as "temporarily unavailable." For anyone who understands modern print-on-demand or POD, this is not truthful. The book is available via print-on-demand within 7 to 10 days regardless of whether it is stored in a warehouse or not.
So why is Dr. Tyson's story unwanted? Why does YouTube and Amazon need to suppress it?
Why exactly or who exactly does not want you or anyone else to get this potentially life-saving treatment?

Fortunately the answers are no longer obscure. This subject was actively discussed by some of the world's leading experts at the Senate Committee Hearing of November 19, 2020.

Dr. Harvey Risch of Yale, Dr. Peter McCullough of Baylor and none other than Imperial Valley's Dr. George Fareed (former Harvard Professor and NIH Virologist) all testified.
Here is the C-span link to the entire 2.5 hour video of the proceedings.

https://www.c-span.org/person/?128373

After you watch this, you will more fully appreciate "The Miracle of the Imperial Valley" and why the story is so threatening to some.

The Desert Review: In Support of Early Outpatient Rx of COVID-19

Originally published in the Desert Review on December 7, 2020

https://www.thedesertreview.com/opinion/letters_to_editor/letter-to-the-editor-in-support-of-early-outpatient-treatment-of-covid-19/article_b342aea6-38b2-11eb-bdf7-8bcbd1e8ade4.html

The Assault Against the People

In response to your recent article about The Assault Against Early Treatment for COVID-19, I would like to offer some comments:

We are witnessing the greatest attack on scholarship and humanity in the last 100 years.
For a society that values science and free speech, history will show that this is one of our darkest episodes. Learned men like our nation's founders, Ben Franklin, Thomas Jefferson, and others, would be ashamed if they were alive today witnessing the corruption of science by our nation's

leading regulatory agencies. If we had only a free and transparent press, the public would hear facts rather than the biased and distorted reporting provided by today's major news sources.

Fortunately at least one publication, *The Desert Review,* has published a factual and credible account of the recent Senate Hearings.

"The Assault Against Early Treatment for COVID-19: How One Congressional Hearing Speaks Volumes about America's Failed Response to the Pandemic," is a feature story authored by Dr. Donald C. Pompan and Dr. Michael M. Jacobs that appeared in the December 03, 2020 edition. In the story, they discuss the remarkable Senate Hearing of November 19, 2020, in which Dr. Fareed, Dr. Risch and Dr. McCullough dominated the scientific argument over the minority expert witness, Dr. Ashish Jha, and concluded that based on overwhelming clinical data that early outpatient treatment of COVID-19 was effective and saved lives.

Unfortunately, the Senate Hearing did not receive adequate media attention, and the little coverage that occurred was shamefully biased by corrupt sources. Among the most blatant was the *New York Magazine* which was reduced to personally attacking Senator Johnson and the esteemed Harvard and Yale physicians.

The New York Times sunk to a new low by publishing Dr. Jha's Op-Ed consisting of a yellow journalistic attack on these Senate Hearings with the title, "Snake-Oil Salesmen of the Senate." If the results of this type of low-class journalism were not so tragic, it would be laughable. Laughable that the *New York Times* would stoop to such depths. But the results are that half a million more people may die because effective treatment is being suppressed.

Misrepresentation of the Senate Hearings: The Fix is In

We are not talking about Hydroxychloroquine. We are talking about effective early outpatient treatment that can spare 2,500 US COVID-19 deaths per day for the next four to six months. We are talking about the effective use of repurposed medicines with proven antiviral properties, medicines like Favipiravir and Ivermectin, in addition to HCQ. These are medicines used as first-line drugs as early outpatient treatments in other countries like Japan, Russia, Greece, and India, where they are faring far better than the US on a per-capita basis.

This is an assault on America. An assault on reason. An assault on humanity.

And it will be revealed in time. Dr. Jha is the doctor who admittedly has not treated a single COVID-19 patient and has not authored a single peer-reviewed publication on the subject. Using these facts, he was humiliated at the November 19, 2020, Senate Hearing by physicians with superior publication records and academic credentials.

Jha then decided to take his revenge by writing a name-calling Op-Ed in the *New York Times* advocating AGAINST a treatment that science shows can save hundreds of thousands of lives between now and the time a vaccine is given to the majority of the US population. Early outpatient treatment is advised by not only Dr. Fareed, Dr. Risch and Dr. McCullough, but by the vast majority of US practicing physicians who employ it for themselves and their family members

What the reader needs to ask is why Dr. Jha cannot refute the studies referenced by the eminent three Ivy League doctors, and why he needs to resort to name calling after the debate. Why did Dr. Jha not say this to their faces during the Senate Hearing? The larger question is why the *New York Times* and the *New York Magazine* wish to suppress a treatment that has been shown to work effectively on an outpatient basis and has been supported in nearly one hundred published studies during a pandemic when hundreds of thousands are dying?

Dr. Harvey Rich edits the *International Journal of Cancer*. Dr. Fareed is the 2015 rural physician of the year for the California Medical Association and holds patents on three cancer drugs. Dr. Peter McCullough holds the senior publication record of all these physicians and serves as the Vice Chair of Internal Medicine at Baylor.

Dr. Jha meanwhile has not treated a single COVID-19 patient or authored a single peer-reviewed publication on COVID-19. He is, however, favored by the media, the FDA and the NIH. He is pushing to wait on a vaccine and advocating zero early outpatient treatment even at the expense of hundreds of thousands of more deaths of people like you and me.

Dr. Harvey Risch writes, "In the future I believe this misbegotten episode regarding hydroxychloroquine will be studied by sociologists of medicine as a classic example of how extra-scientific factors overrode clear-cut medical evidence."

Dr. McCullough describes it as "a crime against humanity."

Dr. Robin Armstrong is the distinguished internal medicine specialist and hospitalist who serves as the medical director for The Resort in Texas City. In this large nursing home, he preserved many lives through his early use of outpatient COVID-19 treatment. He saved 37 of 38 infected patients with this strategy and recommends it become the standard of care in nursing homes throughout the country. He feels that history will not look kindly on physicians who decided to follow the government's ill-advised guidance to withhold early outpatient treatment for their patients.

How kindly will history regard Dr. Jha?

After this pandemic ends, and the science further verifies we could have saved 500,000 US lives if we had only adopted the early outpatient treatment advocated by Dr. Risch, Dr. Fareed, and Dr. McCullough, how will the country react?

Respectfully Submitted,

Justus R. Hope, MD

Author of *Surviving Cancer, COVID-19, and Disease: The Repurposed Drug Revolution*

Chapter 4
THE SECOND SENATE HEARING: ENTER DR. PIERRE KORY

Dr. Pierre Kory Testifies

If Dr. Peter McCullough and crew rankled at Senator Ron Johnson's Homeland Security hearing in November, Dr. Pierre Kory conquered in December.

The Second Senate Hearing: Enter Dr. Pierre Kory

By the time Kory finished his introductory diatribe, the opposition knew they had not buried repurposed drugs, not by a longshot. Kory lit into ranking member Peters punishing him for calling him a political spokesman, and Kory's sincere indignation struck a chord with the listener. Not only did Kory possess the relevant scientific credentials, but he also turned out to be a worthy debater, capable of easily defeating any government-sponsored Dr. Jha.

Big Pharma and the FDA suddenly had to worry.
https://vimeo.com/490351508

The argument was also different than in November. Dr. Kory was talking about a new drug, Ivermectin, not the laughable and easily buried HCQ. The opposition reeled as they reacted to a blindsided attack.

Senator Johnson had not revealed his secret weapon, Pierre Kory until the other side had lowered their guard in overconfidence. The ranking member, Senator Peters, had become so confident that he had left the room, leaving the Johnson witnesses to speak unopposed. Peters did not even put on an opposing expert.
Dr. Kory spoke about "mountains of data" and the "miraculous" effectiveness of Ivermectin. He quoted dozens of randomized controlled studies that supported his statements. Kory proved to be a charismatic and overwhelming presence at the December 8, 2020 Senate Hearings, and his speech jolted the opposition. Kory proved to be the turning point in the war for the human right to access a life-saving repurposed drug.

As the events unfolded over the following weeks, the war was far from won, and there were to be 300,000 more US casualties alone. However, the die had been cast, and the pathway to victory was now evident around the world for Ivermectin and repurposed drugs. Things would never again be the same for Big Pharma and Big Regulators. They had overplayed their hand one time too many, and this time they would get found out.

Dr. Pierre Kory's passionate Senate testimony revealed a study from Dr. Hector Carvallo that showed Ivermectin's 100% effectiveness in a group of 800 front line health care workers compared to a 58% infection rate in the control group not protected with Ivermectin.

In contrast to the November Senate hearings which landed on deaf ears, Dr. Kory's Senate YouTube video went viral, garnering nearly eight million views before the powers that be pulled the plug and took it down for "violating community standards."

Dr. Pierre Kory Champions Repurposed Drugs for COVID-19

Originally published on December 10, 2020

At the Senate Hearing of December 8, 2020, Dr Pierre Kory offered riveting testimony about the effectiveness of repurposed drugs against COVID-19. Dr. Kory has excellent credentials as Pulmonologist and Assistant Clincal Professor at the University of Wisconsin.

Previously, he was a faculty member at the Albert Einstein College of Medicine and the Icahn School of Medicine at Mount Sinai, New York. He is a member of the American College of Chest Physicians and the American Thoracic Society.

An expert on point-of-care ultrasonography, Dr. Kory co-authored a textbook on the subject that was selected for the

The Second Senate Hearing: Enter Dr. Pierre Kory

the British Medical Association's 2015 President's Choice award for medical textbooks. Dr. Kory has also been named to the 2015-2016 Top Doctors in Madison List, was a semifinalist (2009 and 2013) for a Chest Young Investigator Award, was named as a "Rising Star" physician of New York City, and received a Teaching Attending of the Year Award from Mount Sinai Beth Israel.

Ivermectin: The 2015 Nobel Prize in Medicine

At UW-Madison, Dr. Kory has received the James B. Skatrud Teaching Award for Outstanding Teaching in Pulmonary and Critical Care Medicine on behalf of fellows in the Pulmonary and Critical Care Medicine program, and the Outstanding Off-Service Faculty

Teaching Award from the UW-Madison BerbeeWalsh Department of Emergency Medicine.

He cited some 30 studies reviewed by his group that showed that "mountains of data" have showed the "miraculous effectiveness of Ivermectin." It basically "obliterates transmission of this virus. If you take it, you will not get sick."

"Our manuscript which was posted on the Medicine preprint server details this evidence." He cited a recent study from Argentina from the lead Ivermectin investigator in Argentina, Dr. Hector Cavallo. They prophylaxed 800 exposed health care workers with Ivermectin. Not a single of these got sick (with COVID). In the control group of 400 not treated, 58% got sick, some 237 people.

"If you take it, you will not get sick. It has immense and potent antiviral activity."

Dr. Kory further stated that Ivermectin, the remarkable repurposed drug against viruses, has already "won the Nobel Prize for Medicine in 2015" for its effectiveness in parasitic disease. Dr. William C. Campbell, the Nobel laureate delivered the Nobel Lecture, "Ivermectin: A Reflection on Simplicity."

"It is critical for its use in this disease (COVID-19)."

Kory noted that we have more than 100,000 people currently hospitalized and it is essential this drug be used immediately, and be approved by the FDA immediately for emergency and compassionate use for COVID-19.

Senator Johnson agreed to draft a request that the NIH immediately review the data Dr. Kory cited to expedite this approval.

The Second Senate Hearing: Enter Dr. Pierre Kory

Dr. Pierre Kory stated, "I am a physician and a man of science. I have done nothing but commit myself to scientific truth and the care of patients..." He continued, "We are a group of some of the most highly-published physicians in the world. We have nearly 2,000 peer reviewed publications among us."

"We have done nothing but try to figure out to identify a repurposed and available drug to treat this illness (COVID-19) - I am severely troubled by the fact the NIH, the FDA, and CDC - I do not know of any task force that was assigned or compiled to review repurposed drugs in an attempt to treat this disease.

Everything has been about novel and or expense pharmaceutically engineered drugs...we have one hundred years of medicine development. I do not know of a task force that has been focused on repurposed drugs. We (our group) has filled that void. We focus on the things we know and the things we do. We have a solution to this crisis (Ivermectin)."

He declared, "When I am told we are touting things that are not NIH or FDA recommended, let me be clear: NIH, their recommendation on Ivermectin, which is to not use it - is from August - we are now in December - which is three to four months later - mountains of data have emerged from many centers and countries around the world showing the miraculous effectiveness of Ivermectin. It basically obliterates transmission of this virus."

Repurposed Drugs are discussed in the book by Justus R. Hope.

They are effective against terminal cancer and COVID-19. They are, however, unprofitable, and hence, you will not

hear about them from profit-driven media, agencies, and competing interests.
You will hear about them from physicians committed to science and humanity.

https://youtu.be/b9nAp-MjK9I

Dr. Kory's Count: Any Further (COVID) Deaths are Needless: 43,340

Originally published December 12, 2020

The Kory Count Stands at 43,340 needless and preventable COVID-19 deaths as of December 11, 2020.

Dr. Kory, Pulmonary and Critical Care Specialist, and James B. Skatrud Outstanding Teaching Award Winner, stated in his Senate Testimony of December 8, 2020 these words:

"If I have to go back to work next week, any further deaths are going to be needless deaths...I cannot be traumatized by that..I cannot keep caring for patients when I know they could have been saved with early treatment."

He pleaded for the NIH to review his groups' manuscript and volumes of data on the effectiveness of early outpatient treatment for COVID-19 and to provide immediate Compassionate Use approval for physicians to save lives.

"We stand by our manuscript. It is a scientific manuscript. It has been submitted for peer-review. Peer-review takes months. We do not have months. We have 100,000 patients in the hospital now dying. I'm a lung specialist. I'm an ICU specialist. I've cared for more dying COVID patients than anyone can imagine. They're dying because they can't breathe... And I watch them everyday. They die. By the time they get to me in the ICU they are almost impossible to recover. Early treatment is key. We need to offload the hospitals."

Dr. Peter McCullough, Vice Chair of Internal Medicine, and academic powerhouse, delivered a similar message in his Senate testimony on November 19, 2020:

"I'm asking for your help. I'm asking for the government to organize all government agencies to assist doctors in their compassionate care..because we can prevent hospitalization and death, and right now it's the only option on the table."

Dr. McCullough then delivered these prophetic words,

"We are weeks away from mass panic and massive mortality. Labs are hitting 20% positive rates; that means the number of people coming to the lab that are testing positive is 20%, and the average person infects many more; this is a massive calamity that is right around the corner and I'm asking, I'm pleading for the Senate and America right now...to not get clobbered with a tsunami of massive mortality particularly for our elderly citizens."

Did the NIH, FDA and CDC immediately take note? Did they review the data and offer compassionate use guidance so all physicians could immediately employ early outpatient treatment options that have proved so effective (up to 80 to 100 % in saving lives)?

No. We are told our only option is a vaccine that will not arrive in time for most high-risk Americans.

Ivermectin for the World

Meanwhile both Dr. McCullough's and Dr. Kory's predictions are coming true. We are seeing record numbers of cases and (preventable) COVID-19 deaths. If anyone doubts this, please read Dr. Brian Tyson's First Person Account of COVID-19.

With early outpatient treatment, Dr. Tyson saved 1900 infected COVID-19 lives. Only one patient needed to be hospitalized. Listen to the data recited by Dr. Harvey Risch, the eminent Yale Epidemiologist. Read the data on Early Outpatient Treatment published in August in the peer-reviewed *American Journal of Medicine* by Dr. McCullough.

Since November 19, 2020, the following are the horrific numbers of daily deaths that could have been prevented had the government followed the advice of these physician-scientists. The government may not use the excuse they did not know. These words are recorded for the nation in sworn, public, and televised Senate testimony.

Out of respect for the dead, I will continue posting this Kory Count - until such time as the FDA and NIH issue appropriate guidelines - for either Emergency or Compassionate Use of the early outpatient treatment - as advised by Dr. McCullough and Dr. Kory.

<u>Let us be clear</u>: There is no doubt that the benefits of this early outpatient treatment greatly outweigh the risks. There is no downside. These medicines are safe. Hundreds of thousands of lives can be saved from November 19, 2020 forward - or from today forward.

You, the public reader needs to demand this. We doctors have delivered the information. An informed citizenry needs to insist our government implement it.

It is the current US policy to offer zero early treatment to COVID-19 outpatients.

Why in God's name not offer early outpatient treatment with medications proven to kill this virus?

History will judge.

The Kory Count of Preventable Deaths (Updated 12/11/20) with Early Outpatient Treatment:

- November 20: 1952
- November 21: 1429
- November 22: 843
- November 23: 1039
- November 24: 2209
- November 25: 2313
- November 26: 1179
- November 27. 1412
- November 28: 1192
- November 29: 8187
- November 30: 1265

- December 1: 2610
- December 2: 2885
- December 3: 2857
- December 4: 2637
- December 5: 2190
- December 6: 1111
- December 7: 1533

- December 8: 2821
- December 9: 3157
- December 10: 2937
- December 11: 2951

Charley Pride's Sad Loss to COVID-19

Originally published by The Desert Review on December 14, 2020

Anyone who has ever listened to "Kiss an Angel Good Morning" knows who Charley Pride is. He was as American as "Burgers and Fries and Cherry Pies" and the darling of Nashville at a time when his picture was kept off albums because he was black. Regardless of his race, he became country music's first black superstar, the first African American performer to appear onstage at the Grand Ole Opry, and the first to be inducted into the Country Music Hall of Fame.

But Charley also shares a distinction that caused his death. Being African American placed him at higher risk from COVID-19, and this virus caused his death. Progressive physicians like Dr. Peter McCullough from Baylor, Dr. Harvey Risch from Yale, Dr. George Fareed from Harvard, and most recently Dr. Pierre Kory from the University of Wisconsin, have demonstrated the near 100% effectiveness of Early Outpatient Treatment using repurposed drugs - and they have shared this with the nation via Senate Hearings in November and December.

Dr. Pierre Kory, in emotional testimony this week, declared, "You know who's dying here? It's our African American and Latino and elderly. It's some of the most disadvantaged and impoverished members of our society. They are dying at higher rates than anyone else. It's the most severe discrepancy I've seen in my medical career. And we are responsible for protecting those disadvantaged members. We have a special duty to provide countermeasures. The amount of evidence to show Ivermectin is life-saving and protective is so immense, and the drug is so safe. It must be implemented - I'm asking the NIH to review our data and come up with recommendations."

Many doctors who have employed early outpatient treatment have found it to be 100% effective at preventing COVID-19 death - this author included. Dr. Brian Tyson used early outpatient treatment and saved 1900 infected patients. The earlier the treatment is given, the better.
Dr. Pierre Kory stated that any deaths now, knowing that early outpatient treatment is life-saving, are preventable.

The Kory Count is the running tally of the number of COVID-19 deaths that could have been prevented using such early outpatient treatment. Dr. Peter McCullough asked the FDA to approve Early Outpatient Treatment on November 19, 2020. No answer and no approval.

My patients receive it. None have died from COVID. Not a single one of Dr. Brian Tyson's patients who received it died. If Charley Pride had received it, would we be reading about his death today?

I think not.

How many more have to die before the FDA and CDC recognize and provide Emergency Use Authorization and guidance so that ALL physicians can use early outpatient treatment to save their patients? Will our country uphold its duty to protect the most impoverished and vulnerable in our society - our African Americans and Latinos?

Let us all join together and ask - no - let us insist that the FDA review Dr. Kory's data not tomorrow - but today - and issue guidance on early outpatient treatment. The FDA's official policy remains zero early outpatient treatment, which is unacceptable to me, my patients, and their families. It should be unacceptable to you as well.

Today's Kory Count stands at 45,591

The Kory Count of Preventable Deaths (Updated 12/12/20) with Early Outpatient Treatment:

- November 20: 1952
- November 21: 1429
- November 22: 843
- November 23: 1039
- November 24: 2209
- November 25: 2313
- November 26: 1179

- November 27. 1412
- November 28: 1192
- November 29: 818
- November 30: 1265
- December 1:   2610
- December 2:   2885
- December 3:   2857
- December 4:   2637
- December 5:   2190

- December 6:   1111
- December 7:   1533
- December 8:   2821
- December 9:   3157
- December 10: 2937
- December 11: 2951
- December 12: 2251 including Charlie Pride

Kory Count Rises: 61,360 Deaths Now Could Have Been Prevented

Originally published December 18, 2020

Dr. Pierre Kory refers to Dr. Paul Marik as his mentor and "thought leader." Dr. Paul Marik calls it an "International and National Tragedy of Unmitigated Proportions" that no guidelines have been implemented for early and prophylactic treatment for COVID-19. He declares that many of today's pandemic deaths are "needless deaths" and that there are "things we can do right now."

Dr. Paul Marik

Dr. Paul Marik is an internationally-renowned Critical Care Specialist who says, "What we have done is follow the science." He is board-certified in Internal Medicine and Pulmonary & Critical Care Medicine as well as Chief of Pulmonary & Critical Care Medicine at the University of Virginia Medical School. He has authored over 400 peer-review articles, 50 book chapters, and four Critical Care

Textbooks. He also trained as a pharmacist and nutritionist.

He is internationally renowned for his scientific contributions to the treatment of Sepsis.

Dr. Marik and the Front Line COVID-19 Critical Care Working group have developed the I-Mask + Protocol for Early Outpatient Treatment and Prophylaxis using vitamin supplements + Ivermectin. He also discussed the Long-Haulers Syndrome, the chronic condition associated with long-term consequences of the disease.

Ivermectin is well-tolerated and has been prescribed billions of times around the world since 1985. It has potent anti-viral effects, and in particular, interferes with Sars-CoV-2 replication.

Although the US regulators have not recently reviewed the data, The W.H.O. is seriously reviewing his data. Dr. Marik notes that the FDA and NIH promote Remdesivir which does NOT reduce mortality; however Ivermectin DOES REDUCE mortality. Dr. Marik calls upon the FDA/NIH/WHO to "do the right thing" and provide emergency guidance to basically say that "Ivermectin is safe" and that the benefits in treating COVID-19 outweigh the risks.

Dr. Marik points out that the PCR test is notoriously inaccurate and that COVID-19 remains a clinical diagnosis. If a patient tests negative for COVID-19 yet has positive symptoms and X-ray findings, they likely have the disease and should be treated.

Dr. Marik recommends the vitamin supplement cocktail made up of Vitamin D3, Vitamin C, Quercetin, Melatonin and Zinc as a general supplement cocktail for most people, especially everyone at high risk.

The Second Senate Hearing: Enter Dr. Pierre Kory

For those who have been exposed, Dr. Marik advises early treatment with Ivermectin (prescribed by a physician) in addition to the supplements.

Dr. Marik discussed both pre-exposure and post-exposure prophylaxis using Ivermectin.

Dr. Marik cited a study that found that those individuals living with a COVID-19 family member had a 30 to 50% chance of contracting the disease; however if they were given Ivermectin, their chances dropped to 7%.

He cited another study [Carvallo H, et al. J. Biomed Res Invest 2020;2:1007] showing zero of 788 health care workers getting infected who took Ivermectin preventatively, while a control group of 407 untreated saw 237 workers get infected (58%).

Out of 21 studies, 100% show positive results with Ivermectin. It is effective in all stages of the disease, in early treatment, late treatment, pre-exposure prophylaxis and post-exposure prophylaxis.

Dr. Marik notes that without FDA guidelines most US physicians will not prescribe Ivermectin for COVID, either for prevention or treatment.

Clearly the weight of data around the world shows that Ivermectin is universally positive in helping prevent and treat COVID-19.

"We need more data to get conventional drug approval. Clinical trials are in progress." However, due to the emergency nature of this pandemic the FDA can and does provide for EUA, Emergency Use Authorization as they did for Remdesivir, which does not save lives.

"Remdesivir has minimal or no impact on the course of this disease, and indeed the W.H.O. no longer recommends the use of Remdesivir for the treatment of COVID...Unfortunately the bias of the NIH and our health care authorities is for the treatment of the hospitalized patient. They have completely ignored the enormous impact we can have on this disease by prevention and early treatment."

In stark contrast, Ivermectin has been shown through numerous observational studies to save lives by preventing the disease and impacting it in the early phases. It should be accorded EUA - immediately.

"There are interventions we can do right now to prevent getting this disease."

We could be stopping the majority of current daily deaths by implementing this early treatment.
What does Dr. Paul Marik do for himself? What does he do to protect himself? "When I am working in the ICU, I do not want to get COVID-19. I take 15 mg of Ivermectin and I wear a mask." Dr. Marik takes 2,000 IU of Vitamin D per day. I take 4,000 IU per day.

My high risk patients receive the benefit of early outpatient treatment. We have not had a single COVID-19 death. Dr. Brian Tyson's treated all 1900 of his COVID patients, and lost no patients. Only one got sick enough to be hospitalized.

Meanwhile, the deaths in the US are rising to record levels, and we are averaging a 9/11 death toll [3,000] every day. We are averaging a Vietnam War Casualty level [50,000] nearly every two weeks.

Most patients are not receiving any early outpatient treatment despite the recommendations made at the Senate

The Second Senate Hearing: Enter Dr. Pierre Kory

Hearings by World-Class Medical Experts like Dr. Harvey Risch, Dr. George Fareed, Dr. Peter McCullough, Dr. Pierre Kory, and now Dr. Paul Marik.

How will our country react if God-forbid, we learn in the future that half a million deaths could have been prevented if the FDA had enacted Emergency Use Authorization in December of 2020?

I do not feel it will come to that. I believe that reason will prevail over greed and censorship.
The last time I wrote the Kory Count Preventable Death number was at 45,591 as of December 12, 2020.

Dr. Kory asked the NIH to review his data in his December 8th testimony to the Senate Committee on Homeland Security chaired by Ron Johnson. A formal request was sent to the NIH to review his group's mountain of data.

"Their silence has been deafening," states Dr. Marik. There is more needed than just a vaccine. We need early outpatient treatment NOW, until the vaccine can be administered - which can take many more months.

Will America continue to sit by and passively watch the daily media one-two drumbeat - panic and overwhelmed hospitals followed by the Vaccine Panacea - while we lose 80,000 more Americans every month?

Or will we do the right thing - add early outpatient treatment - provide EUA guidance for all physicians to use repurposed drugs - as a complementary strategy - to save hundreds of thousands of lives now - while we wait for everyone to receive the vaccine.

As a result of failure to issue guidance on Early Outpatient Treatment we now adjust this Kory Count number upward:

- December 13 deaths. 1357
- December 14 deaths. 1678
- December 15 deaths. 3025
- December 16 deaths. 3611
- December 17 deaths. 3293
- December 18 deaths. 2805

CURRENT KORY COUNT = 61,360 and rising while the NIH remains silent on reviewing Dr. Kory's data.

WE NEED AN ANSWER FROM THE FDA/NIH TODAY.

"We need to engage and inform physicians so they are less reluctant to prescribe Ivermectin. Patients need to know there is an option. The public has an option. We need to inform physicians that this treatment Ivermectin has 30 years of treatment that is safe and effective. Hopefully the FDA and W.H.O. will be supportive." says Dr. Marik.

Let us all rally around Dr. Kory and Dr. Marik to get the FDA/NIH/W.H.O to provide Emergency Guidance to approve Ivermectin for early outpatient treatment.

Get this message out.

We cannot afford any more preventable COVID-19 deaths!

Dr. Paul Marik Transforms Sepsis & COVID Care with Vitamin C

Originally published December 26, 2020

Anyone who has followed repurposed drug development knows two things:

> *Repurposed Drugs are a threat to regulators and Big Pharma as they can subtract from their profits (by effectively treating disease for which more expensive drugs are designed)*

> *The well-funded interests will quickly design studies attempting to call the effectiveness of the repurposed drug into question; i.e., they will design a study to make the repurposed drug fail (use it at an improper dose, or at a time it predictably will not work)*

To illustrate these points let me tell you about Dr. Paul Marik and his innovative use of ascorbic acid in sepsis treatment.

Septic shock is a disease seen in the ICU and carries a high mortality rate; that is: most patients rapidly die regardless of any drugs you throw at it.

Such was the case in one of Dr. Marik's ICU patients about three years ago. Marik explains that this patient rapidly worsened and developed kidney and heart failure. She was already intubated on a mechanical ventilator when this happened. Dr. Marik knew she would be dead within 24 hours.

He did what caring and innovative doctors do. He thought outside the box and recalled a study he had read. It had to do with high dose Vitamin C infusion in a septic patient. Dr. Marik read the study and realizing that Vitamin C was safe and non-toxic, decided to give her the infusion.

He left the hospital that evening, fairly certain his patient would either be dead or dying when he returned the next morning. However, to his amazement, her kidneys had suddenly begun making urine, and her failing heart was recovering. She was extubated that morning and was able to leave the hospital a few days later with a full recovery.

Naturally, Dr. Marik decided to try this again the next time he was faced with a dying and septic patient. It worked again, and then again, and then again. He decided to publish his results to the world could use this strategy to save lives.

His landmark study, "Hydrocortisone, Vitamin C, and Thiamine for the Treatment of Severe Sepsis and Septic Shock," was published in Chest on February 3, 2017.

DOI:https://doi.org/10.1016/j.chest.2016.11.036

In a group of 47 controls with Septic Shock, the death rate was 40.4 % in the standard-of-care group. In the Vitamin C group, the mortality rate was 8.5%. There was over 80% less chance of death when the patients were given Vitamin C.

Not surprisingly, the NIH and others did not share the enthusiasm for these results. In an NIH-funded study, Vitamin C was given late and at a different dose. These patients were given the Vitamin C ONLY AFTER they

The Second Senate Hearing: Enter Dr. Pierre Kory

developed ARDS, known as a death sentence. With the wrong dose given at the wrong time, this may have been designed to fail. However in spite of all else it succeeded!

The standard of care group had a death rate of some 45 % while the Vitamin C group's was 29%.
In another study known as the VITAMINS study in Australia, there was no data on time between admission and randomization. Dr. Marik noted that one must administer the Vitamin C within 6 hours of admission to be effective.

He contends waiting more than 18 hours increases the chance of death. Marik condemned the VITAMIN study design as "ethically and morally unacceptable." It was a study designed to refute Dr. Marik's results.

The Marik protocol has been adopted by ICU physicians worldwide.
Dr. Marik reasoned that Sepsis and COVID-19 Cytokine Storm patients are similar in that both die very frequently and there is no known treatment. So he did the logical thing. He used a similar "Marik Protocol" with them. And guess what?

He achieved very similar success. In the recent peer-reviewed paper just published in the Journal of Intensive Care Medicine by college Dr. Pierre Kory, entitled, "Clinical and Scientific Rationale for the "MATH+" Hospital Treatment Protocol for COVID-19," Dr. Kory described the success of this protocol.

I quote, "The average hospital mortality at these 2 centers in over 300 patients treated [Marik Protocol] is 5.1%, which represents more than a 75% absolute risk reduction in mortality compared to the average published hospital mortality of 22.9% among COVID-19 patients."

Naturally there are some that are not thrilled about this. *Medscape* writes, "Doctors Publish Paper on COVID-19 Protocol; Experts Unconvinced."

However, most practicing physicians welcome any non-toxic treatment that can reduce the death rates by 75% or more. Most practicing physicians applaud Dr. Marik, as do all of the patients whose lives he has saved.

However, some do not. You already know who they are.

Chapter 5

FROM ACROSS THE POND: DR. ANDREW HILL JOINS THE FRAY AND THE NIH REACTS

Dr. Andrew Hill dropped a bombshell on December 27, 2020 when he joined the supporters of Ivermectin.

Dr. Andrew Hill gave an excited and sometimes breathless interview with French media via YouTube describing his meta-analysis of the Ivermectin data stating that Ivermectin appeared "transformative."

The bombshell was not that Dr. Andrew Hill was a highly regarded Oxford graduate MD, PhD and marathon athlete. It was not even that Dr. Hill had done extensive work as a virologist for large pharmaceutical Goliaths like GlaxoWellcome and Roche. It was not that he was on the editorial board of AIDS and the current editor of The Journal of Antimicrobial Therapy. It did not involve the fact he ran a charity which supports children with HIV/AIDS in Thailand.

The real kicker was that Dr. Andrew Hill, senior visiting Research Fellow in the Pharmacology Department at Liverpool University, was working with UNITAID, an official arm of the WHO that received vast funding from the Bill and Melinda Gates Foundation.

It appeared on its surface that Ivermectin was on the verge of obtaining an approval from the World Health Organization – something that formerly seemed impossible given the entrenched politics.

Excitedly Dr. Hill announced that if the data he found were confirmed, a WHO approval should be forthcoming by the end of March. In a further and unexpected development, the trio of Dr. Paul Marik, Dr. Pierre Kory, and Dr. Andrew Hill were invited to the offices of the US National Institutes of Health to give a presentation of their data on Ivermectin's effect on COVID. This presentation, against all odds, took place on January 6, 2021, and all eyes focused on the NIH's response.

From Across the Pond: Dr. Andrew Hill Joins the Fray

Indeed, the NIH reacted by changing their guidelines and admitting that the trio's data had served to update their last recommendation which was from August 27, 2020.

The FLCCC issued an official press release that read,

On January 6, 2021, Drs. Pierre Kory and Paul Marik, founding members of the **Front Line COVID-19 Critical Care Alliance (FLCCC)**, appeared before the **National Institutes of Health COVID-19 Treatment Guidelines Panel**.

The panel, which is in the process of reviewing the rapidly emerging data on the role of ivermectin in the prevention and treatment of COVID-19, invited Drs. Kory and Marik to present the latest data, along with Dr. Andrew Hill—a senior research fellow at the University of Liverpool, who was hired by UNITAID to provide research for the World Health Organization (WHO).

The NIH invited the FLCCC members and Dr. Hill to the panel to present the four months of data on ivermectin that has emerged since the NIH last issued its guidelines on August 27. During the meeting, the FLCCC and Dr. Hill pressed the NIH to reevaluate their recommendation for ivermectin.

The doctors explained to the panel that numerous clinical studies—including peer-reviewed randomized controlled trials—showed large magnitude benefits of ivermectin in prophylaxis, early treatment and also in late-stage disease. Taken together, the doctors reported that the dozens of clinical trials that have now emerged from around the world are substantial enough to reliably assess clinical efficacy.

Specifically, the FLCCC physicians and Dr. Hill presented data from 18 randomized controlled trials that included over 2,100 patients. The trial results demonstrated that ivermectin produces faster viral clearance, faster time to hospital discharge, faster time to clinical recovery, and a 75% reduction in mortality rates.

"In order to save thousands who will die while waiting for their turn to receive the vaccine, it is imperative that treatment guidelines issued by the NIH over four months ago be updated to reflect the strength of the data for Ivermectin in prophylaxis, early treatment, and late-stage disease," said Dr. Kory, FLCCC president, following the hearing.

The NIH panel signaled their intention to consider the data and anticipates an update to their current recommendations by early February.

The aftermath was not quite as expected. The NIH revised their guidance on Ivermectin from against to neutral, that is they felt the data was insufficient to recommend either for or against its use in COVID-19. Nonetheless the NIH, a US agency, now found itself at odds with its fellow FDA, and this conflict would be noticed by the world.

How could science provide contradictory conclusions. Afterall, only lawyers and politicians are supposed to disagree about the interpretation of facts. Scientists should agree on true scientific data, especially world-class WHO scientists.

It would get even worse later when Dr. Andrew Hill suddenly became silent, and UNITAID was accused of changing his report. Later, Dr. Tess Lawrie, also a consultant to the WHO would also speak out. Eventually, it would appear that Big Pharma and Big Regulators could not possibly plug all the leaks at the same time. It seemed the Ivermectin coverup could no longer be maintained. But before the dam would burst, hundreds of thousands more lives would be lost. Ultimately lawyers would join the fight for the human right to medical treatment.

WHO-Scientist Calls Ivermectin a Potential "Transformational Treatment"

Originally published January 3, 2021

Dr. Andrew Hill of the Department of Pharmacology at The University of Liverpool has released preliminary results of a WHO-sponsored analysis of 11 randomized clinical trials of Ivermectin involving 1452 in-hospital participants from around the world. These are the results: Ivermectin was associated with:

* Faster time to viral clearance
* Shorter duration of hospitalization
* 43% higher rates of clinical recovery [95% C.I. 21-67%]
* 83% improvement in survival rates [95% C.I. 65-92%]

Dr. Hill speaks of Ivermectin in this video as a potentially transformational treatment. He says that now the only questions are the optimal dose and how many days it should be taken.

https://youtu.be/yOAh7GtvcOs

Currently, the study is reviewing 56 trials totaling some 7,100 patients, and Dr. Hill is waiting for three more to release results. Meanwhile, the U.S. predicts some 115,000 more American deaths from COVID-19 to occur in January - at least 83% of these are now preventable with in-hospital Ivermectin with even more preventable with earlier outpatient treatment.

* The U.S. has the power through the CDC/NIH to issue Emergency Use Approval of Ivermectin today to save these lives. Who is responsible for failing to answer Dr. Kory's December 8, 2020, Senate plea for the NIH to review the Ivermectin data?

https://youtu.be/Tq8SXOBy-4w

Dr. Peter McCullough, Dr. George Fareed, and Dr. Harvey Risch have been calling for such early outpatient treatment since the first Senate Hearing held November 19, 2020. It is unconscionable that the NIH fiddles while COVID kills.

* Why has the NIH failed to answer while hundreds of thousands more die, while our hospitals run out of capacity, and while our economy crumbles?
* When will the NIH speak about Ivermectin?

The Kory Count of Preventable COVID-19 deaths is once again updated:
The beginning Kory Count as of December 30, 2020: 90,187

December 31: 3462
January 1:   1917
January 2:   2373

Today's Kory Count of Preventable COVID-19 Deaths: 97,939

NIH Holds Hearing with Dr. Kory, Dr. Marik, and Dr. Andrew Hill

Originally published January 7, 2021

The NIH has finally taken the first step towards Emergency Use Authorization of Early Outpatient Treatment by inviting Dr. Pierre Kory, Dr. Paul Marik and WHO Senior Fellow Dr. Andrew Hill to present data. On January 6th, these three physicians summarized the results of 18 peer-reviewed and randomized controlled trials that included over 2,100 patients showing benefits of Ivermectin in the treatment of COVID-19 in all stages of the disease - from prophylaxis, to early stage and also in late-stage illness.

Their results showed large magnitude benefits with early viral clearance, faster time to hospital discharge, and a 75% reduction in mortality rates.

"In order to save thousands who will die while waiting for their turn to receive the vaccine, it is imperative that treatment guidelines issued by the NIH over four months ago be updated to reflect the strength of the data for ivermectin in prophylaxis, early treatment, and late-stage disease," said Dr. Kory, Front Line COVID-19 Critical Care Alliance, FLCCC president, following the hearing.

The FLCCC Alliance was organized in March, 2020 by a group of highly published, world renowned Critical Care physician/scholars – with the academic support of allied physicians from around the world – to research and develop lifesaving protocols for the prevention and treatment of COVID-19 in all stages of illness.

Ivermectin for the World

FLCCC ALLIANCE

The Frontline Covid19 Critical Care Alliance

Dr. Paul Marik | Dr. G. Umberto Meduri | Dr. Jose Iglesias | Dr. Pierre Kory | Dr. Joe Varon

Dr. Eivind Vinjevoll | Dr. Scott Mitchell | Dr. Keith Berkowitz | Dr. Howard Kornfeld | Dr. Fred Wagshul

Their **MATH+ Hospital Treatment Protocol** – introduced in March, 2020, has saved tens of thousands of patients who were critically ill with COVID-19. Now, the FLCCC's new **I-Mask+ Prophylaxis and Early At-Home Outpatient Treatment Protocol** with Ivermectin has been released – and is a potential solution to the global pandemic. https://covid19criticalcare.com/

The NIH panel signaled their intention to consider the data and update their recommendation but did not give a date for their decision.

In this blog, we have attempted to keep the reader updated on all the latest developments with Early Outpatient Treatment using repurposed drugs. We have followed the Senate Hearings involving Dr. Peter McCullough who published the seminal study on Early Outpatient Treatment and testified on November 19, 2020 along with Harvard and Yale experts Dr. Harvey Risch and Dr. George Fareed. Dr. Kory followed up with testimony at the second Senate Hearing held on December 8th, 2020 asking the NIH for expedited review of the overwhelming world-wide data showing the effectiveness of such treatment.

From Across the Pond: Dr. Andrew Hill Joins the Fray

Finally, Dr. Andrew Hill announced preliminary results of a WHO-sponsored meta-analysis of 11 studies recently causing him to describe Ivermectin as a potentially transformative treatment.

The Kory Count has been published regularly on this site out of respect to the preventable deaths from COVID-19.

I am saddened to say the NIH has not yet provided EUA for either Ivermectin or Early Outpatient Treatment which would greatly decrease these ongoing daily deaths.

Although it is a positive step the NIH has made in holding the January 6, 2020 hearing, every day that the NIH delays in issuing the Emergency Use Authorization means thousands more foreseeable and preventable deaths.

On January 6, 2020, the day of the hearings, the U.S. saw 3,964 daily deaths. Soon the number will surpass 4,000 per day - unless the NIH issues the EUA - and the sooner the better. What are they waiting for?

The beginning Kory Count as of January 2, 2020: 97,939

- January 3: 1,353
- January 4: 2,048
- January 5: 3,689
- January 6: 3,964

Today's Kory Count of Preventable COVID-19 Deaths: *108,993*

Cardiologist Cures 99.3% of 7,000 COVID Patients Using Ivermectin

Originally published January 9, 2021

Dr. Redondo Saves Lives With Ivermectin

Reprinted from DOMINICAN TODAY, November 30, 2020

This article does not constitute medical advice, and any decision to embark on medical treatment must be done with the careful supervision and prescription of a patient's personal physician.

After eight months of active clinical observation and attending about 7 thousand patients of Covid-19 in three medical centers located in Puerto Plata, La Romana, and Punta Cana, Dr. José Natalio Redondo revealed that 99.3% of the symptomatic patients who received care in his emergency services, including the use of Ivermectin, managed to recover in the first five days of recorded symptoms.

The renowned cardiologist and health manager affirmed that Ivermectin's use against the symptoms of Covid-19 is practically generalized in the country and attributed to this factor, among others, the fact that the risk of dying from this disease in the Dominican Republic is significantly lower than in the United States.

The also tourist businessman and founder of the National Network of Medical Services RESCUE GROUP said he had found that the most significant impact and the real intervention to vary the results were in VIROSIS's early management.

He added that "in a therapeutic format duly tested over the years, infections have always been cured faster and leave fewer sequelae if antimicrobial treatment is applied as early as possible since this allows the use of lower doses of the selected drugs. This has been one of the dogmas that remain in our daily medical practice."
The key is early treatment.

After pointing out that early treatment should be the goal, Dr. Redondo maintained that Ivermectin could be the effective instrument to prevent that bridge of progression from being installed, with very harmful results, even if the patient does not die.

The physician with more than 40 years of practice of medicine presented a report on the experience registered in the clinical management of Coronavirus in the health establishments ascribed to the RESCUE GROUP, integrated by the Bournigal Medical Center, of Puerto Plata; Clinica Canela, of La Romana; and Punta Cana Medical Center, in the province of Altagracia, where about seven thousand patients diagnosed with the virus have been attended since last March 2020.

"From the beginning, our team of medical specialists, who were at the forefront of the battle, led by our emergency physicians, intensivists and internists, raised the need to see this disease in a different way than that proposed by international health organizations, says Dr. Redondo in his report.

And he adds that the Group's experts proposed the urgency of reorienting the management protocols towards earlier and more timely stages. "We realized that the war was being lost because of the obsession of large groups, agencies, and companies linked to research and production of drugs, to focus their interest almost exclusively on the management of critical patients.

"Our results were immediate; the use of Ivermectin, together with Azithromycin and Zinc (plus the usual vitamins that tend to increase the immune response of individuals) produced an impressive variation in the course of the disease; it was demonstrated that 99. 3% of the patients recovered quickly when the treatment was started in the first five days of proven symptoms, with an average of 3.5 days, and a fall of more than 50% in the rate and duration of hospitalizations, and reducing from 9 to 1 the mortality rate, when the treatment was started on time."

Integral management of Covid-19

Dr. José Natalio Redondo explained that "once the presence of the virus was demonstrated in our areas of influence, three of our hospitals were adapted to a process of physical re-engineering and management to turn them into Health Centers authorized for the integral management of COVID-19 patients."

He indicated that at that time, an expanded committee was also created to design, supervise and evaluate an Institutional Management Guide for patients with COVID-19, "following the guidelines established by the Ministry of Health of our country, the Dominican Republic, and the management protocols imposed on us by the international accreditation held by our hospital Centro Médico Punta Cana with Canadian accreditation."

"This committee consists of more than 20 medical professionals, specialized in Critical Care and Emergency Medicine, internists, infectious pneumologists and epidemiological researchers from several countries, among others, who have met every Thursday of each week, since mid-April, to update and modify the Management Guide so that it can serve as a binding instrument for the professional practice of our associated physicians, and especially our residents of the specialties of Emergency Medicine and Critical Care or Intensivists."

High rate of hospitalization and mortality

He emphasized that this committee was the promoter of the use of Ivermectin in the management of the disease associated with Covid-19; "first of all, because of the evident inefficiency shown by the management schemes initially proposed by national and international organizations, which were filling our hospitals with seriously ill patients and a very high mortality rate.

And later, because of the impressive information published by the group of researchers led by Caly and his collaborators, about the almost miraculous effect of the old and very well-known antiparasitic and antiviral drug "Ivermectin," in the elimination of the burden of the coronavirus 2, cultivated in laboratory Vero Slam cells, in Monash University, Australia," points out Dr. Redondo.

He specifies that Dominican patients were dying mainly because of the loss of time in seeking rapid medical assistance, or because of the inconsistent policy of sending them home, without antiviral treatment, with paracetamol and hydration, until their evolution led them to get worse so that they returned to the emergency service.

"Those who get complicated have a common denominator that we see repeated and repeated, always, they arrive when the inflammatory phase has already begun; at a time when the immune response can be so intense that it attacks our cells, or when the damage caused by the virus at the intracellular level is already almost irreversible," Dr. Redondo emphasizes.

57 Physicians Call for Early COVID Treatment While Deaths Skyrocket

Originally published January 13, 2021

Dr. George Fareed Calls for Early Outpatient Treatment to Save Lives

COMMENT: The 01/11/21 Press Release is reprinted from PRNewsWire. Yesterday the U.S. Deaths from COVID-19 rose to a new daily grim milestone: 4,406. As the following article reveals MOST could have been prevented with early outpatient treatment with combinations of safe and well-known drugs such as ivermectin, hydroxychloroquine, azithromycin, doxycycline, and favipiravir (outside the US). It is tragic that our leadership has suppressed this life-saving information. Please print out this news release and show it to your doctor. It could save yours or another's life.

***

BRAWLEY, Calif., Jan. 11, 2021 /PRNewswire/ -- Widely available outpatient treatments can reduce COVID-19 illness severity, hospitalization and mortality when used early in the disease, according to a new peer-reviewed article co-authored by Dr. George Fareed, MD, Medical Director of Pioneers Health Clinic, and 56 other doctors and academics in a special COVID-19 issue of *Reviews in Cardiovascular Medicine*.

With vaccines taking time to deploy and having only partial success in high-risk patients, these early outpatient therapies can help manage the disease by lowering mortality and reducing the burden on overstretched healthcare systems.

The outpatient therapies include combinations of widely available drugs and nutraceuticals (zinc, vitamin D, vitamin C, quercetin) as well as anti-infectives, steroids and anticoagulants if necessary. The new protocol features FDA-approved antibody infusions manufactured by Lilly and Regeneron, which are available at hospitals and should be available at urgent care centers and nursing homes soon.

Widely available treatments can reduce COVID-19 illness severity, hospitalization and mortality when used early.

For patients who do not receive antibodies, early sequential multidrug therapy (SMDT) calls for combinations of well-known, safe drugs such as ivermectin, hydroxychloroquine, azithromycin, doxycycline, and favipiravir (outside the US), along with inhaled steroids such as budesonide and oral steroids including dexamethasone and prednisone.

The article notes that dozens of countries around the world are already using these drugs for early outpatient treatment of COVID-19, including some like Brazil and India which are widely distributing ivermectin and hydroxychloroquine in at-home treatment kits.

Addressing the debate over drug efficacy, the authors note that trials producing claimed null findings suffer from serious flaws including unblinded protocols, absence of placebo controls, changing endpoints, and truncated sample sizes.

By contrast, ongoing reviews and meta-analyses of over 200 studies of hydroxychloroquine and 44 studies of ivermectin suggest early use of these drugs in combination with others results in substantial reductions in disease severity, hospitalization, and mortality.

The article emphasized the safety of these drugs, which have been safely used by hundreds of millions of people around the world. Regarding hydroxychloroquine for COVID-19 specifically, a study in the European Society of Cardiology's journal, *EP Europace*, concludes, "HCQ administration is safe for a short-term treatment for patients with COVID-19 infection regardless of the clinical setting of delivery."

Citation:

McCullough, Peter, et al. "Multifaceted highly targeted sequential multidrug treatment of early ambulatory high-risk SARS-CoV-2 infection (COVID-19)." *Reviews in Cardiovascular Medicine*, 2020, Vol. 21, Issue (4): 517-530. DOI: 10.31083/j.rcm.2020.04.264

Contact:

Harvey A. Risch, MD, PhD
Professor of Epidemiology
Yale School of Public Health
Yale School of Medicine
Yale Cancer Center
Harvey.Risch@Yale.edu

The ICON Study: Dr. Jean-Jacques Rajter Reviews Ivermectin

Originally published by Dr. Hope on January 18, 2021, this article contains references to Dr. Jean-Jacques Rajter's Senate Testimony, along side Dr. Pierre Kory delivered on December 8, 2020.

Dr.Rajter Saves COVID-19 Lives with Ivermectin

As always, there are those who will argue with study results. Especially those who have a vested monetary interest.

When Dr. Rajter showed convincingly that Ivermectin effectively saved lives in his COVID-19 patients, certain groups were less than pleased. His early results showed that the sickest and ICU patients had less than 1/2 the rate of death with Ivermectin compared to those without it.

The naysayers argued that the groups were not evenly matched, and that the Ivermectin group received more steroid which can improve survival. However in the following statement that Dr. Rajter made to the Senate, this cannot explain the difference.

Without further comment, I reprint Dr. Jean-Jacques Rajter statement below. You be the judge.
***

US Committee on Homeland Security and Governmental Affairs
Early Outpatient Treatment: An Essential Part of the COVID-19 Solution, Part II

Prepared statements by:
Jean-Jacques Rajter, MD
Pulmonary, Critical Care, and Sleep Specialist Pulmonary and Sleep Specialists Florida
1001 S. Andrews Ave, Suite 100
Fort Lauderdale, FL 33316

Honorable Senators of the Committee on Homeland Security,

My name is Jean-Jacques Rajter, MD.

It is an honor and privilege to stand here in front of this committee providing first-hand experience on the early treatment for COVID-19. I am a pulmonary, critical, and sleep specialist residing in Broward County, Florida. My practice, Pulmonary and Sleep Consultants of Florida is made up of myself, my wife and business partner Dr. Juliana Cepelowicz Rajter, 2 full time Advanced Registered Nurse Practitioners, and 1 part time Advanced Registered Nurse Practitioner. We have a thriving inpatient and outpatient practice providing care to thousands of patients annually.

My team has extensive experience with treatment of COVID-19 in both inpatients and outpatients.

Although the first human cases of COVID-19 were originally reported in Wuhan in December of 2019, the first confirmed US cases of COVID-19 were in mid-January. It was not until March were confirmed cases of COVID-19 started appearing in Florida. Early on in the pandemic, most US physicians and health care facilities were caught off guard, as no proper diagnostic testing, protective equipment, and treatment algorithms were readily available.

During that first wave of COVID-19, hydroxychloroquine based regimens were considered appropriate, as no alternative options had been proven to be effective. I am not here to debate the merits or short comings of hydroxychloroquine based regimens, as this has already extensively been done by all parties involved.

By early April, it became quite apparent that those hydroxychloroquine regimens did not work well in patients with more advanced COVID-19, as many of them ended up in ICU on ventilators and subsequently died.

In early April, Dr. Kylie Wagstaff and a team of researchers at Monash University in Australia published data indicating that Ivermectin was effective at reducing COVID-19 viral loads by 5000 fold within 48 hours in their cell culture models.

The very next day, a COVID-19 patient of mine was rapidly deteriorating. She had gone from room air, to nasal cannula, to 50% oxygen over a few hours and was continuing to deteriorate.

From Across the Pond: Dr. Andrew Hill Joins the Fray

She would likely be intubated shortly with its associated high mortality. After discussing her care with her family, I was implored to look for any other possible alternative to avoid further clinical deterioration. The patient's son was literally pleading with me to find some alternative to save his mother's life. We discussed the results of the in-vitro study using Ivermectin.

Even though the drug has a great safety record, the patient's son was advised that no dosing trials had been completed. After extensive discussion we agreed that Ivermectin had other approved indications and he requested that I attempt use of an approved dosing regimen. Since no other options were available at the time, informed consent was obtained and Ivermectin administered.

The patient deteriorated as expected for about 12 more hours, but stabilized by 24 hours and improved by 48 hours. Subsequent to this, 2 more patients had similar issues and were treated with the Ivermectin based protocol.

Based on past experience, these patients should have done poorly, yet they all survived.
This laid the foundation for the ICON study (Use of Ivermectin is Associated With Lower Mortality in Hospitalized Patients With Coronavirus Disease 2019) which was peer reviewed and published in CHEST, a major US based medical journal.

Even though I did a lot of peer reviewed published research in my earlier years, I am currently a clinical physician who prior to this pandemic had no interest or inclination to do further research. Yet, I could not stand idly by as I have seen more people die in the past 6 months than I have in my entire medical career combined.

Extraordinary times called for extraordinary measures.

The ICON study is a retrospective propensity matched observational study looking at the effect of ivermectin on hospitalized patients. Propensity matching is aimed at reducing the likelihood of selection bias and reducing the effects of confounding variables. Our propensity matched pairs were assessed based on age, gender, pulmonary condition, hypertension, HIV status, severe pulmonary disease at presentation, exposure to steroids, hydroxychloroquine, azithromycin, race, WBC count, absolute lymphocyte count, and need for mechanical ventilation at the time of study entry.

We were limited to enrolling 300 patients into the study based on the limitation imposed on us by the Institutional Review Board. 107 patients received conventional care and 173 patients received conventional care plus Ivermectin.

The overall mortality was 25% in the conventional care, whereas it dropped to 15% in the Ivermectin treated group. This was statistically significant difference in favor of Ivermectin use. In those patients with severe pulmonary disease at onset, the mortality benefit was even more staggering at 80.7% versus 38.8%. We concluded that further studies were needed to confirm those preliminary findings.

My team has multiple study protocols in place, ready to be implemented in short order. We have established relationships with international teams to complete such randomized controlled trials, yet funding for such studies has been elusive at best.

During the second wave of the pandemic, it was common for my team to treat in excess of 40 patients with COVID-19 on a daily basis. This ICON protocol has been optimized over the months as more information regarding treatment successes and failures became apparent. The success rate of the Ivermectin based protocol is now far superior to what it was in its early days. The current ICON protocol is as follows:

- Ivermectin 200 mcg/kg orally on day 1 and 2. May redose on day 8 and 9, 15, 22, and 29 as needed if patients remain symptomatic.
- Doxycycline 100 mg orally twice daily for 5 days or azithromycin 250 mg orally daily for 5 days if unable to take doxycycline.
- Vitamin C 1000 mg twice daily.
- Vitamin D3 1000 units daily.
- Zinc sulfate 220 mg daily or 50 mg of elemental zinc daily.
- Famotidine 20 mg twice daily.
- Atorvastatin 40 mg daily.
- If hypoxic dexamethasone 6 mg daily for 10 days.
- If mildly hypoxic, will need supplemental oxygen at home.
- If D dimer elevated, will need anticoagulation.
- If more severe and requires hospitalization, will consider convalescent plasma transfusion x2 and remdesivir with or without baricitinib.

Ivermectin based protocols have now been studies across the world, yet no major large scale randomized control study has been completed. A meta-analysis of 21 studies looking at the effectiveness of Ivermectin in COVID-19 was released on November 26. The results of this study is attached below.

This included: 3 early treatment studies from Espitia-Hernandez, Carvallo, and Cadegiani. 12 late treatment studies from Gorial, Podder, Khan, Chachar, Mahmud, Rajter, Hashim, Camprubi, Elgazzar, Spoorthi, Budhiraja, and Niaee. 4 pre-exposure prophylaxis studies from Behera,

Carvallo, Hellwig, and Bernigaud. 2 post exposure prophylaxis studies from Shounan and Elgazzar

Some detractors of Ivermectin use point to the fact that Wagstaff and team used supratherapeutic levels of Ivermectin in her cell lines.

They obviously miss the fact that the original study in cell lines was merely a proof of concept and not a dosing trial. Subsequent studies completed by the very same research team in lung cells indicated that a cumulative dose of 350-450 mcg/kg would achieve effective tissue levels of Ivermectin.

<u>We came to the same conclusion based on clinical experience and have been a 200 mcg/kg on 2 consecutive days dosing regimen since May. Of the hundreds of outpatients treated by my team, only 2 were admitted to the hospital, one due to heart failure, the other due to symptomatic delay of over 1 week before seeking medical attention.</u>

Neither of them died, neither of them needed intubation.

Detractors of Ivermectin use would also point to some fabricated or extravagant safety concerns for Ivermectin use. Ivermectin is widely used with in excess of 3.7 billions doses administered wordwide.

It is part of the WHO efforts to eliminate onchocerciasis and lymphatic filariasis as a public health problem in much of Africa. In APOC countries (Angola, Burundi, Cameroon, Central African Republic, Chad, Congo, Democratic Republic of Congo, Ethiopia, Equatorial Guinea, Gabon, Kenya, Liberia, Malawi, Mozambique, Nigeria, Rwanda, Sudan, Tanzania and Uganda), it is estimated that 65% of the total population living in an endemic area need to take ivermectin annually to eliminate onchocerciasis and lymphatic filariasis as a public health problem.

It is currently also approved for treatment of strongyloidiasis and scabies. Because of this, Ivermectin is part of the WHO Model List of Essential Medications.

The ICON dosing regimen is based on a currently accepted dosing regimen for Norwegian scabies. This dosing regimen has long standing safety data. Safety of a medication is due to its pharmacokinetics and possible interactions, but not its intended use. Hence, these safety concerns are significantly exaggerated.

Remdesivir for example is known to cause renal insufficiency and failure, yet has been considered the standard of care. Yet no study has documented a survival benefit for this medication.

As of November 20, the WHO recommends against the use of remdesivir in COVID-19 patients. WHO has issued a conditional recommendation against the use of remdesivir in hospitalized patients, regardless of disease severity, as there is currently no evidence that remdesivir improves survival and other outcomes in these patients.

As is the case with any infections, early intervention has been proven time and again to be of critical importance. The same is true for COVD-19.

> Early intervention increases the likelihood of keeping people out of the hospital and hence decreasing the pressure on the Health Care system.
>
> Early intervention is cost effective as it decreases the overall Health Care expenditure.
>
> Early intervention and treatment decrease viral shedding and viral transmission in the home

setting which is currently believed to me a major site of transmission.

Early intervention increases survival.

Early intervention decreases the economic impact. Other treatment modalities have also not shown to be extremely effective. As discussed above, remdesivir has not been shown to impact mortality. Convalescent plasma has not been widely documented as improving survival either. Steroids improve survival by several percentage points only.

Even if vaccines are 80% successful (debatable but subject of another senate hearing I'm sure), we still need to treat the 20% of people who become ill with COVID-19 notwithstanding vaccination. Some people may not be able to receive the vaccine for a variety of reasons. Vaccines may not be widely available for many months. Vaccines may not provide long term immunity. Based on these factors, treatment for COVID-19 will need to remain on the forefront even after vaccination programs are initiated.

To summarize, based on the facts as presented above, Ivermectin is effective in early disease, late disease, post exposure prophylaxis, and pre exposure prophylaxis. The response to Ivermectin has been well documented. Ivermectin is an oral medication requiring no monitoring. It is safe and has a long track record of such safety. It is inexpensive and widely available.

From Across the Pond: Dr. Andrew Hill Joins the Fray

The US has spent billions of dollars on a multitude of treatment options. My team is ready to proceed with the needed randomized control trials to address any such residual doubt related to Ivermectin use. Yet we are unable to proceed due to lack of funding and support.

A few hundred thousand dollars, may definitively proof or disprove the effectiveness of Ivermectin for early treatment with a properly designed and implemented randomized control trial. More funding could look at the effectiveness of pre and post exposure prophylaxis using Ivermectin. A couple million dollars could complete a multi-center double blind, placebo control trial with Ivermectin.

Based on the John Hopkins COVID Resource Center, our beautiful country has over 266,000 people dead to date with a mortality of 82 people per 100,000 population. Norway and Finland have a mortality of 6.2 and 7.2 per 100,000.

If this were extrapolated to the US, our mortality to date would only be 20 to 23,000 people. Australia with 3.6 per 100,000 would extrapolate to 12,000.

Ladies and gentlemen, I implore you as a front line provider of COVID-19 to do better. To provide us the answers we need as health care providers to help your constituents survive this horrible pandemic in great number. May God bless you and the United States of America.

As Dr. Rajter suggests, the data is overwhelmingly in favor of using Ivermectin now to save lives. It is cheap, it is safe, and as of this writing 18 randomized controlled studies involving 2,100 patients have confirmed the benefits of Ivermectin treatment in all stages of COVID-19.

Every day we delay in getting the Emergency Use Authorization from the NIH to use Ivermectin results in an average of 3,000 to 4,000 more "needless deaths" to use Dr. Pierre Kory's words.

For the sake of humanity, let everyone you know hear about Ivermectin so they can bring it to their physician's attention.

Chapter 6
IVERMECTIN GOES TO COURT

Ivermectin Goes to Court & The NIH Relaxes its Prohibition

After the two Senate Hearings, the gloves came off. It became a race to get the vaccine out before the truth about Ivermectin got out. The ends justified the means according to the opposition. And getting everyone vaccinated as soon as possible meant that the preventable deaths could be swept under the rug.

If the pandemic could be contained, then the FDA, CDC, and NHS could come out smelling like a rose, and no one would be the wiser. The profit machine could continue, and repurposed drugs could continue to be marginalized.

But no one saw Ralph Lorigo coming. Not even the repurposed drug proponents. However, his cases would change the landscape of the debate. Because you cannot censor court decisions, at least not effectively. That meant the powers that be had to ignore these cases, and when publicity happened, they had to drown them out with volume.

Notice that at first Ivermectin was ignored. This happened back in December after Dr. Kory testified. Later, when his Senate video spread to eight million views, they took it down. When Lorigo's first court case showed that his client recovered from a ventilator with Ivermectin, and that made headlines, they knew they needed to take a different approach.

So they pretended to embrace the research. They invited Dr. Kory and two others to "present" their evidence to the NIH. They feigned impartiality. And then they ruled. The data were too strong. So they split the baby and upgraded their guidance to neutral. It did not hurt Remdesivir or the vaccine push. It made them appear fair.

However, what they didn't plan on was a second Lorigo case with the same benefit and then a third. They had to do something more to neutralize the Ivermectin data. Ultimately, they managed to influence a lone study in South America to serve their cause. But these legal cases would continue to plague them. They continued to censor and provide conflicting "news." They continued to manufacture doubt about science when none existed. They continued to confound and confuse, much like Big Tobacco did for decades, before the truth was found out by the public.

Judith Smentkiewicz Wins Court Order for Life Saving Ivermectin

*Originally published in The Desert Review
January 16, 2021*

https://www.thedesertreview.com/opinion/letters_to_editor/ivermectin-goes-to-court-and-the-nih-relaxes-its-prohibition/article_440b7300-59bf-11eb-b945-4f69ec28f4c0.html

On January 14th, the National Institutes of Health revised its guidance on Ivermectin and removed the recommendation against its use for COVID-19. Based in part upon review of data presented by Dr. Pierre Kory and Dr. Jean-Jacques Rajter in the December 8th Senate Hearings on Early Outpatient Treatment for COVID-19 and Dr. Kory's testimony delivered directly to the NIH panel on COVID-19 January 6th, 2021, the NIH acted.

In my opinion, they did not act enough. Although the NIH no longer recommends against using Ivermectin for COVID-19, they do not recommend for its use. More mothers and grandmothers are dying BECAUSE the NIH has not taken the added step of including Ivermectin in its Emergency Use Authorization.

Accordingly, I am today updating the Kory Count, the number of "needless deaths" to use Dr. Kory's words that could have been prevented had the NIH, with the stroke of a pen, accorded Ivermectin EUA status.

The story below shows how 80-year-old grandmother and mother Judith Smentkiewicz had her life saved by Ivermectin, no thanks to her hospital and no thanks to the NIH. Her life was saved in spite of the hospital, and the hospital attorney's fight against her use of Ivermectin. They lost in court, and she won in life.

Judith was given Ivermectin while on mechanical ventilation in the ICU. She responded to the Ivermectin rapidly, going off the ventilator and leaving the ICU within 48 hours. Her recovery was in line with the scientific data – in particular, it was typical of the ICON Study results published in the journal *CHEST* by Dr. Jean-Jacques Rajter in Broward County, Florida. His sickest ICU cases responded best to Ivermectin with less than ½ the death rate of those without the Ivermectin.

Ivermectin prevents COVID-19 deaths.

The Judith Smentkiewicz story is told by her son and her lawyer, Ralph C. Lorigo in the attached video:

https://youtu.be/qanytFQbwW0

However, the Kory Count shows that fully 140,139 preventable deaths have occurred in the United States since November 19th, 2020, when Dr. Peter McCullough first advocated in the Senate for Early Outpatient Treatment, including the use of Ivermectin.

The Kory Count of Preventable Deaths is Updated:

Beginning number from November 19th through January 7th: 113,105

Current Kory Count of Preventable COVID-19 Deaths: *140,139*

Ivermectin Goes to Court Again and The Kory Count Reaches 170,000

Originally published in The Desert Revie
January 27, 2021

Since the NIH adjusted its guidance on Ivermectin to neutral on January 14th, another 32,590 souls have perished. Based on the evidence produced by Dr. Andrew Hill of the WHO, some 83% of these deaths could have been prevented had the NIH instead revised this guidance to "Recommend."

We are looking at so many preventable deaths that I share Dr. Kory's disgust. Dr. Kory announced to the Senate on December 8th, 2020, that any further deaths are needless because the benefits of ivermectin are now known. I keep track of the Kory Count out of reverence to the dead and to keep it known that these deaths were preventable.

Ivermectin for the World

The court case where Judith Smentkiewicz's son had to hire an attorney and get an injunction to force the hospital to provide her ivermectin underscores the problem our country faces. My patients and their families all enjoy the protection of ivermectin because my practice provides education and access.

About 10% of other physicians do the same for their patients. The vast majority of doctors do not, and their patients face COVID-19 alone or with research done by family members like Judith Smentkiewicz's son. She was lucky to survive, and one can read her story in "Ivermectin Goes to Court."

Her attorney, Ralph Lorigo, saved her life.

It is not every day that an attorney is able to save a life, but Mr. Lorigo did so when he obtained a court order for the hospital to administer ivermectin to Ms. Smentkiewicz. She was a single mother who went above and beyond to raise her two children by herself. She worked as a secretary and later cleaned houses four days a week so her children could survive. Her son repaid the favor when the ICU physician told him his mother would probably die. At age 80 and on a ventilator with COVID, the chances were 80% that the virus would take her life. But her son went above and beyond, and he found an article that suggested ivermectin could help her, and the rest is history.

Of course, the naysayers will argue that this was anecdotal at best. And that it did not prove that ivermectin works. However, the pesky proverbial fly in the ointment is that it happened a second time to Glenna Dickinson, and the same lawyer, Ralph Lorigo, decided to help her family. He went to court and got a second judge also to issue a court order to force the hospital to administer the ivermectin, and she also improved. Judith Smentkiewicz set a legal precedent that others are now following.

So in who's Brave New World are we now living where rich pharmaceutical companies call the shots, and doctors and regulators can be bought? You and I are expendable resources in a society where the truth and morals no longer matter. We have seen scientific studies falsified on a large scale and published in the most respected journals. Dr. Hector Carvallo, a leading researcher on ivermectin, says the biggest problem with ivermectin is that it is cheap. Large pharmaceutical companies and the US want nothing to do with a drug that cannot make money.

I now update the Kory Count in the hopes that my message may, by some miracle escape the bounds of censorship, and that somehow it may find its audience of Americans who will decide to follow Judith Smentkiewicz's lead and obtain an avalanche of similar court-orders, to allow doctors everywhere to prescribe effective and repurposed drugs for COVID-19 before we lose half a million more lives.

Dr. Peter McCullough has published extensive guidelines about ivermectin and sequential multi-drug therapy for COVID-19. A brochure has been published by the American Association of Physicians and Surgeons that can be obtained for free that lists physicians and resources to help patients. Dr. Pierre Kory's group, the FLCCC, can offer direction to anyone seeking to utilize ivermectin.

Attorney Ralph Lorigo has shared his legal papers with other lawyers across the country seeking assistance with court-ordered ivermectin.

The Kory Count of Preventable Deaths is Today Updated:

Beginning Kory Count November 19th through January 15: 140,139

Current Kory Count of Preventable COVID-19 Deaths: **172,729**

COVID Recovery from the ICU in 48 Hours: A Lawyer uses Ivermectin

Originally published January 30, 2021

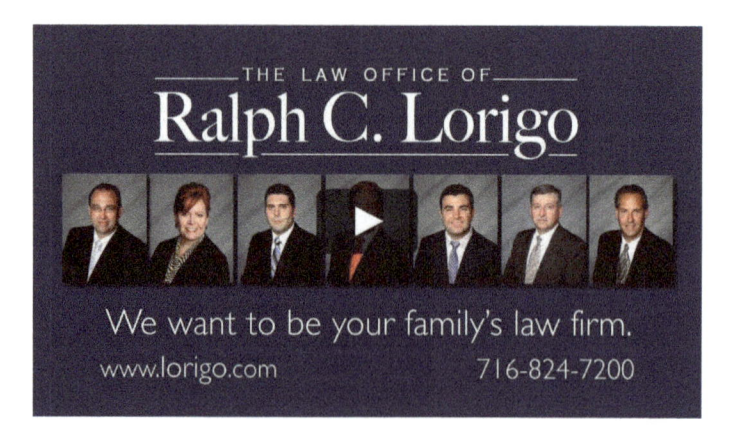

The Law Firm of Ralph C. Lorigo

"The only thing a lawyer can do is bring a lawsuit." But attorney Ralph Lorigo has already saved multiple people from COVID. He may have saved more lives from COVID than some physicians.

His cases involving Judith Smentkiewicz and Glenna Davidson have already made national news.

Lorigo obtained a judge's order compelling Millard Fillmore Hospital of Buffalo, New York to administer Judy the Ivermectin. After Ivermectin, she rapidly improved going off the ventilator and leaving the ICU within 48 hours. She left the hospital, recovered some five days later.
Glenna rapidly improved, yet remains in the hospital. Since the publicity, attorney Lorigo has received telephone

calls and emails from all over the country. He receives 40 to 50 emails per day and has reached out to many families and other attorneys seeking help in obtaining Ivermectin.

Lorigo gave a podcast interview and told his remarkable story of the unbelievable opposition that the hospital and hospital attorney gave.

In a January 28, 2021 podcast that was broadcast by Heartland.org, Anne Marie Scheiber interviewed lawyer Ralph C. Lorigo, who soon would lead the nation in winning Ivermectin court-orders against obstinate hospitals which refused to administer the life-saving drug.

Even after the court order for Judith Smentkiewicz, the Buffalo Hospital would not accept the physician's verbal prescription for the court-ordered Ivermectin. The family physician - who normally never cares for hospitalized patients - was forced to drive to the hospital and physically walk the prescription in before they would give Judy the drug.

Mr. Lorigo has worked on two additional cases in other states, where he provided paperwork to the local lawyers.

The California case was dramatic. A husband fought to get Ivermectin for his wife. After getting the lawyers involved, they agreed to provide it. However, her COVID was late stage to the point the husband was summoned to say his final good-byes. Dr. Pierre Kory had consulted with the patient's doctor who agreed to pressure the hospital to allow it.

There is a dramatic report and timeline.

Lorigo tells the story, "They agreed for the Ivermectin. But the hospital called him saying 'you better come in because she is dying.' He hadn't been able to go there, but because she was dying, they let him in."

"And he gives this report hour by hour, how she is holding on, he's holding her hand, he's praying, and he spends the night. And the next morning at 11:00 am, they finally bring the Ivermectin. At 7:00 pm everything changes; her blood pressure goes back up, things are stabilizing."

She's not out of the woods yet as this happened only yesterday.

"It's just incredible," he says. He also helped another woman whose father was hospitalized in Mississippi. They were able to convince the hospital to allow it without court intervention. "Now he's got the Ivermectin."

That's the first rule: "You have to be an advocate. You need to be an advocate. There needs to be an advocate. You never see these people (the hospital officials). It's over the phone."

Attorney Lorigo refers to the Senate Testimony given by Dr. Pierre Kory about Ivermectin. This compelling and passionate speech delivered by Dr. Kory has been viewed by almost 10 million - It has successfully evaded the censorship now all so common among repurposed cheap drugs. Many were inspired by Dr. Kory's speech to ask about Ivermectin for their loved one.

Kory has already been invited by and spoken directly to the NIH to speed up Ivermectin's approval. "I believe Ivermectin will soon become the standard of care in this disease (COVID-19)."

Lorigo says that he and Dr. Kory have worked together in helping many gain access to this life-saving medication.

Attorney Lorigo invites anyone who needs his help to email him, "Look I'm willing. It's an easy email, its Rlorigo@lorigo.com. I am willing to give information. You need to be an advocate."

Ralph Lorigo is a true hero at a time when good doctors find ourselves at odds with the hospitals, the regulators, the media, and the pharmaceutical companies in our attempt to preserve lives in this Pandemic.

As readers of my site have seen, there are many reasons cheap, repurposed drugs are shunned, despite the fact they save lives.

They are shunned for use in cancer, and they are shunned for use against COVID-19, not because they don't work, and not because the science doesn't support them, but mainly because they are unprofitable.

YouTube Censors the Senate: The Canary in Our Coal Mine

Originally published by the Desert Review February 2, 2021

The Canary Speaks

Senator Ron Johnson wrote this OP-ED in the Wall Street Journal on February 2nd, 2021.
Below is an excerpt:

"Google's YouTube has ratcheted up censorship to a new level by removing two videos from a US Senate committee. They were from a Dec. 8th Committee on Homeland Security and Governmental Affairs hearing on early treatment of Covid-19. One was a 30-minute summary; the other was the opening statement of critical-care specialist Pierre Kory.

Dr. Kory is part of a world-renowned group of physicians who developed a groundbreaking use of corticosteroids to treat hospitalized Covid patients. His testimony at a May Senate hearing helped doctors rethink treatment protocols and saved lives.

At the December hearing, he presented evidence regarding the use of Ivermectin, a cheap and widely available drug that treats tropical diseases caused by parasites, for prevention and early treatment of Covid-19. He described a just-published study from Argentina in which about 800 health-care workers received Ivermectin and 400 didn't. Not one of the 800 contracted Covid-19; 58% of the 400 did.

Dr. Kory asked the National Institutes of Health to review his group's manuscript outlining dozens of successful trials and to consider updating its Aug. 27th guidance in which it recommended "against the use of Ivermectin for the treatment of Covid-19, except in a clinical trial." On Dec. 10th, Sen. Rand Paul and I sent a letter to the NIH requesting that it review Dr. Kory's evidence."

Allow me to add my comment and voice to Senator Johnson's.

Since the request was made to the NIH, they, to their credit, invited Dr. Andrew Hill, Dr. Pierre Kory, and Dr. Paul Marik to travel to Bethesda and speak to their committee on COVID-19 treatment on January 6th.

As a result, the NIH broke ranks with the FDA. They removed the restriction against Ivermectin instead raising their guidance to "neutral" and according it the same status as polyclonal antibodies. This has paved the way for Ivermectin to become widely used in the pandemic by informed patients and informed physicians.

However, censorship now blocks this vital and lifesaving information from reaching the public.
When I wrote my book attempting to help my friend survive his brain cancer and drawing upon my 38 years of experience and knowledge as a practicing physician, it never occurred to me that certain powerful interests would not want my message to reach readers. It never occurred to me that censorship still takes place in the US.

However, with the blatant removal of critical care specialists' Senate testimony, that is exactly what is happening now.

The larger question is "Why?"

Why should you not be allowed to hear the testimony of scientists who were qualified and invited to speak before the US Senate?

Why should cancer patients not be able to read the material in my book, "Surviving Cancer COVID-19 and Disease: The Repurposed Drug Revolution"?
Why do we allow de facto censorship in the US, and what are the potential future effects of such censorship?

You may believe that YouTube is a kind, generous titan that exists to serve humanity, and its goal is make certain that you listen to only the best and clearest scientific evidence. If you feel this type of parental filtering serves your interests, perhaps you would be willing to purchase some ocean front property in Arizona.

Like me, if you are skeptical, and believe there is a more sinister motive, be alarmed, be vocal, and object to censorship because censorship is merely the canary in the coal mine. If you see them dropping dead all around you, you should take heed.

America needs to awaken and realize that our parental agencies and captains of industry are not behaving in our best interests; instead, they are catering to theirs. When the number of preventable US deaths exceeds 200,000, perhaps someone needs to sound the alarm.

Accordingly today I update the Kory Count out of respect for those precious lives lost in the pandemic, those lives that could have been saved with the early outpatient treatment discussed by Dr. Pierre Kory in his Senate testimony that YouTube has now banned.

Dr. Pierre Kory, Dr. Peter McCullough, Dr. Harvey Risch, Dr. George Fareed, Dr. Jean-Jacques Rajter, and other visionaries all testified before Senator Ron Johnson's Homeland Security Committee, and their message must be amplified, not censored. With early outpatient treatment, we can save up to one hundred thousand lives per month, beginning immediately.

Such early outpatient treatment, starting with adding Ivermectin both for prevention and treatment, will save countless precious lives, and they may be those of you, your family or your loved ones.

Tell everyone you know about the canaries in our coal mine. Most importantly, inform those who run the mine that something needs to be done before it is too late. Bring a stop to the escalating Kory Count.

The Beginning Kory Count: November 19th through January 15th: 170,809

Current Kory Count of Preventable COVID-19 Deaths Through February 1st
190,893

"Drill Sergeant" Credits Ivermectin with Saving His Life

Originally published February 14, 2021

Courtesy of FLCCC

Actor Louis Gossett Jr. won an Academy Award for his performance as Gunnery Sergeant Emil Foley in the 1982 film "An Officer and a Gentleman."

He played a tough taskmaster with a heart in that role.

In real life, Louis Gossett Jr. recently endured the toughest role of his life when he contracted COVID-19. He explains that an "angel" came to him and told him about Ivermectin. He learned more about it through Dr. Pierre Kory's FLCCC website, and took the medication.

He recovered from the illness, and he credits Ivermectin with saving his life.

Recently YouTube banned Dr. Kory's Senate testimony video which had gone viral with some eight million views.

Louis Gossett Jr's video can be seen below.

https://youtu.be/AsZal-fc8o4

Dad Dies While Awaiting Ivermectin Approval

*Originally published in the Desert Review
March 5, 2021*

Herman van de Westhuizen was a father of three and grandfather to five

Herman van de Westhuizen died two weeks after his application for Ivermectin was not approved. He had been battling the virus for four weeks and waiting for the Ivermectin for two.
Like the families of Judith Smentkiewicz and Glenna Dickinson, Herman's family also found a physician willing to prescribe the Ivermectin. They had to first get the drug approved under the compassionate use exception in South Africa, which had been promised "within 24 hours."

Dr. Naseeba Kathrada wrote the prescription and assisted with the Section 21 application. Then the waiting period began. The virus ravaged Westhuizen's lungs as his application stalled. His family watched helplessly as the pandemic claimed another life.

Tanya Johnson lost her father, Herman van de Westhuizen, on January 31, 2021, to COVID-19, just two weeks after the Ivermectin was prescribed, and two weeks after the application to SAHPRA was made.

Johnson told a reporter, "I can't say that he died because we couldn't get the Ivermectin, but they should have just given us the chance. We went through all the right channels, and I didn't go and buy Ivermectin on the black market."

She summarized the Ivermectin situation in South Africa, "It's like, no matter how much money you have, it just doesn't seem to matter. If they don't want to respond to you, you've got no power over it. There's nothing you can do."

Ivermectin continues to be an unregistered product according to SAHPRA, the South African Health Products Regulatory Authority, their version of our FDA. However, doctors there can apply to access the drug if they submit a proper application.

In January, after mounting pressure from medical doctors, SAHPRA approved Ivermectin in a controlled, compassionate use program that required completion of a Section 21 application.
When asked if she would file another Section 21 application if another family member were to contract COVID-19, Johnson said this: "I would rather buy it on the black market than try to go through that again."

She has taken legal action against SAHPRA and the Minister of Health in a case filed before the Pretoria High Court.

South Africa's obstacles to Ivermectin access seem remarkably similar to those in America.

The family of Judith Smentkiewicz had to deal with her hospital's refusal to honor a valid prescription of the drug. Her story made national news when her son hired a lawyer and took Millard Fillmore Suburban Hospital to court where a judge issued a court order compelling the hospital to follow her doctor's advice to administer the Ivermectin.

It turned out to be lifesaving. Judith had been in intensive care, on a ventilator, and appeared to be on her deathbed. Her family was warned she had only a 20% chance of survival. Within 48 hours of the first Ivermectin dose, she was off the ventilator, breathing on her own, and discharged from the ICU. Her attorneys, Ralph C. Lorigo and Jon F. Minear, have been credited with saving her life. Others have given credit to New York Supreme Court Judge Henry J. Nowak, who ruled against the hospital.

In *The Citizens Voice* on February 1, 2021, Joseph Dupont wrote: "The judge once again saved this woman's life. After all, we can't hinder high body counts to give comfort and hope to us citizens. We must be coerced to take relatively untested vaccines rushed to the market."
Judith is now back at home and recovered from her ordeal with COVID-19 and the court battle. She told reporters that she had no memory of the events. "I had no idea that any of this was going on," she told the Buffalo News. "My son and daughter didn't tell me the whole story until I got home."

She recalls being taken to the hospital in an ambulance and being placed on a stretcher in a hallway. "I know they put me on the ventilator that day, but I don't remember a single thing that happened until January 4th when I was taken off the ventilator."

In a second similar case, Glenna Dickinson's family also won a court order compelling the hospital to administer the Ivermectin to her, with similar improvement.

Dr. Pierre Kory and Dr. Jean-Jacques Rajter spoke before the US Senate in December, imploring the NIH to review the mountains of emerging data, all showing the beneficial effects of ivermectin against the virus.

This resulted in the NIH upgrading their guidance on the drug. Other countries around the world have also recognized the benefits of the drug. Ivermectin is now approved for the treatment of COVID-19 in Zimbabwe, Bulgaria, Slovakia, and Macedonia. It is widely used in South America.

Dr. Andrew Hill and Dr. Tess Lawrie believe it may soon receive WHO approval.
However, there has been a move to suppress its use in the United States. It is rarely mentioned positively in the mainstream press, and many have accused the social media of censoring anything positive to do with repurposed drugs. Recently YouTube took down a video of Dr. Kory's Senate Testimony about Ivermectin.

In South Africa, similar to the US, hospitalized patients cannot receive the treatment, despite a physician's order, unless they take the issue to court.

A group of 50 physicians has joined Tanya Johnson in the legal action against SAHPRA and their Health Minister. The group wrote in court papers that many of its members want to use Ivermectin themselves as a prophylactic and obtain it from a reputable and recognized supplier.
In a recent court ruling, the North Gauteng High Court issued an order to enable doctors to start treatment immediately along with the submission of the Section 21

application. Sadly, the ruling was not in time for Herman van de Westhuizen.

Dr. Naseeba Kathrada led the charge for early outpatient treatment of COVID-19 in South Africa, and has written an open letter to President Cyril Ramaphosa in this regard.
  This has been remarkably similar to the movement started by Dr. George Fareed in the United States when he penned a similar open letter to Dr. Anthony Fauci on August 11, 2021. Fareed's full letter is reprinted in the book, *Surviving Cancer, COVID-19, and Disease: The Repurposed Drug Revolution.*

Dr. Fareed and his associate, Dr. Brian Tyson made national news with their success using early outpatient treatment. Dr. Fareed's letter sparked a Congressional Inquiry that led to two Senate Hearings and the beginning of widespread awareness of early outpatient treatment.

Tragically this awareness has not translated into widespread availability resulting in hundreds of thousands of preventable COVID deaths. Dr. Fareed and his group of 56 highly respected academic physicians published their peer-reviewed article on the early outpatient treatment protocol in a special issue of Reviews in Cardiovascular Medicine:

https://rcm.imrpress.com/EN/10.31083/j.rcm.2020.04.264

And most unfortunately, Dr. Fauci has not yet responded to Dr. Fareed's open letter despite being provided with a copy of it delivered by the Senate liaison to the NIH. Dr. Fareed and Dr. Tyson were recently featured on an interview in which they described their Early Outpatient Treatment model and their record of successfully treating 5,000 COVID-19 patients with only 2 deaths.

https://youtu.be/6o4chAS1N9M

Ivermectin Wins Landmark Court Battle

*Originally published by The Economic Standard
March 26, 2021*

The legal war for access to the life-saving drug Ivermectin is being waged both in the United States and South Africa. The US battle is led by Buffalo, New York attorney Ralph C. Lorigo while Bongani Luthuli fights in Johannesburg. Mr. Lorigo made national news when he won a court order two months ago forcing Millard Fillmore Suburban Hospital to administer the Ivermectin that saved Judith Smentkiewicz's life from COVID-19. Within 48 hours of her first Ivermectin dose, she was taken off the ventilator and able to breathe on her own.

Attorney Lorigo and his associate, Jon F. Minear, won another similar Ivermectin court injunction for patient Glenna Dickenson later in January. Mr. Lorigo has led the charge for patient access to Ivermectin in the US. He now corresponds with scores of other patients worldwide and provides legal and medical resources to access the treatment.

In an interview with the Heartland Institute, Mr. Lorigo recounted his experience with Judith Smentkiewicz's family.

"They were very positive about Dr. Pierre Kory and his group. They gave me a video clip of Dr. Kory in front of the US Senate in December of 2020. It's such a passionate plea. I did so much research. I've got so much of the paperwork. I've expanded our (legal) research substantially since then because we've gotten calls from all over the country, in fact, all over the world about this situation. We handled a second lady in a neighboring county in Rochester, New York. We were able to get a second court order to help her."

After witnessing firsthand the results of these two cases and scores of others he has helped indirectly, Mr. Lorigo has become a steadfast supporter of Ivermectin treatment for COVID. He is available for consultation and assistance at rlorigo@lorigo.com. Mr. Lorigo is clear, "People need to know there is an alternative. They need to know Ivermectin is potentially a miraculous drug for a lot of people. We need to get the word out on Ivermectin because people are dying every day."

Tragically, Dr. Kory's video was taken down by YouTube, and most patients remain in the dark regarding Ivermectin. This censorship has been chronicled in the book *Surviving Cancer, COVID-19 and Disease: The Repurposed Drug Revolution*, in a feature story, "YouTube Censors the Senate and Bans Dr. Pierre Kory."

Meanwhile, in South Africa, SAHPRA, the African equivalent of the US FDA, has opposed access to Ivermectin. The story of Herman van de Westhuizen was published March 5, 2021 in the Desert Review, "Dad dies while awaiting ivermectin approval."

Herman contracted COVID-19 and his family requested Ivermectin. Dr. Naseeba Kathrada wrote the prescription and filed the Section 21 compassionate use application. Unfortunately, SAHPRA delayed the application's approval, and Mr. van de Westhuizen died from the virus two weeks later.

His daughter, Tanya Johnson, joined in the lawsuit against SAHPRA and the Minister of Health. Attorney Luthuli says the Section 21 process is "frustrating and completely unworkable." Although both sides had filed legal paperwork for a hearing set for the end of the month, a settlement was reached this week.

Bongani Luthuli announced earlier this week that SAHPRA's lawyers had agreed to all their requests. "Due to the pressure of the ACDP and others, they've conceded the usage and rollout of Ivermectin. They will be registering the product Wednesday (March 17, 2021)."

"It is a major breakthrough for the people of South Africa because we've been very adamant that Ivermectin can assist in this pandemic. This is now a settlement as opposed to a directive from the court."

However, as with all legal proceedings, the devil proved to be in the details. The settlement means the Ivermectin is now registered in South Africa, and it can be produced by in-country compounding and using only in-country ingredients. The problem is that the importation of any pills or ingredients involved in the compounding would still require Section 21 approval.

Practically speaking, it would be nearly impossible to meet the South African Ivermectin demand without gaining an additional waiver from the Minister of Health to import these key ingredients.

Meanwhile, around the world, the pandemic rages out of control despite aggressive vaccine rollouts. Hungary, despite mass vaccination, has seen cases up almost tenfold since last month. Europe is experiencing a third wave despite millions having been vaccinated, while troubling signs are cropping up in the United States. Forbes staff writer Nicolas Reimann published an article on March 18, 2021 in which he noted that the states with the highest vaccination rates were starting to spike in case counts.

He cited an Axios analysis that found Michigan leading the way in new cases with a 7-day rolling average spike of 53%. Since Axios performed the analysis, the trend has continued. Compared to February 21, Michigan's cases have risen on average from 1030 per day to 4122 per day – a quadrupling.

State health officials blame this increase on contagious new variants spreading within Michigan. Other states with high vaccination rates include West Virginia, Maine, and Montana, and they are dealing with similar spikes. US health officials have conceded that the UK variant could become the dominant strain in our country by the end of the month. It is 56% more contagious and up to twice as lethal than the original strain.

The variants are a significant problem for many reasons, but the most compelling is that they are more resistant to our vaccines. According to an article published March 9, 2021, in WebMD by Ralph Ellis, Pfizer and Moderna vaccines do not work as well against the South African variant (B.1.351), although they still appear effective against the UK variant (B.1.1.7).

Citing a study published in *Nature*, he reported that the percentage of neutralizing antibodies for the South African variant was 12.4 fold lower for the Moderna vaccine than against the original and 10.3 fold lower for the Pfizer vaccine. A 12.4 fold reduction equates to a 92% reduction in effectiveness, while a 10.3 fold reduction equates to a 90.3% lowering.

In another study published March 16, 2021, in the New England Journal of Medicine, the AstraZeneca vaccine was evaluated against the South African variant and found to be only 10.4% effective. William Haseltine, a contributor to Forbes, wrote, "This is cause for grave concern as the South African variant shares similar mutations to the other variants."

Dr. Peter McCullough was asked his thoughts on this serious issue.

Dr. Peter McCullough, distinguished epidemiologist and Vice-Chair of Internal Medicine at Baylor in Dallas, is well-known in the pandemic, largely from his testimony as a lead witness from the first Senate Hearings delivered in November of 2020 during which he advocated early outpatient treatment, including the triple therapy of a cocktail consisting of an antiviral, an antibiotic, and Zinc.

He sounded the alarm during this crucial hearing, predicting that the pandemic would soon overwhelm hospital capacity. Dr. Harvey Risch, the distinguished Yale epidemiologist, and researcher cited over 200 studies attesting to HCQ's effectiveness in outpatient COVID-19 treatment. Dr. George Fareed, former Harvard Professor, and NIH virologist, testified to his experience in treating many hundreds of patients in California's Imperial Valley (along with his associate Dr. Brian Tyson) with the triple therapy of HCQ, Zinc, and Azithromycin without a single death. (As of this writing, the two physicians have jointly treated some 5,000 COVID-19 cases with only two deaths.)

Dr. McCullough recently expanded on his Senate testimony during an interview on the Covexit forum.

"Coming into that Senate testimony, I predicted that we were going to overflow our hospitals – if we didn't have early treatment. To overflow US hospitals, we would have to have 135,000 patients in the hospital with COVID. We crested at 128,000 in the United States, and then the rates started to plummet. We had data come in...that as a result of that testimony and then followed up by the second testimony on December 8 by Dr. Kory and others, we think there was a big surge of early treatment in the United States. The AAPS estimates that 500,000 people actually received early treatment. And so that probably changed the face of the pandemic. We started to see mortality, new cases, and hospitalizations go down at the same time."

When asked about today's rising cases and the problem of new variants, Dr. McCullough offered his thoughts: "There was a mindset in the National Institutes of Health that it (the solution) was going to be vaccination against the spike protein and nothing else...The regulatory agency's position is single drug – one by one – and they have not been able to think in a multidrug environment...We have to be adept from a public health perspective in following the science...If our contagion control methods look like they've backfired, and are ineffective, we need to change them. If we are seeing a mortality signal with a vaccine, and we really see this, we don't want to whitewash that. We want to have independent reviews."

One independent review has already been accomplished. Dr. Tess Lawrie is the director of the Evidence-Based Medicine Consultancy in Bath, England. She is routinely called upon by the British National Health Service and the World Health Organization to perform comprehensive and independent meta-analyses on medical evidence. Her results inform decisions in making international guidelines on clinical practice.

Dr. Lawrie performed such a comprehensive analysis on the medical evidence with Ivermectin. Dr. Lawrie concluded, "Between Christmas and new year, I independently reviewed 27 studies presented by the FLCCC as evidence of Ivermectin effectiveness. The resulting evidence is consistent and unequivocal: Ivermectin works well both in preventing COVID infections and in preventing deaths at the same doses used to treat lice and other parasitic infections.

I am very pleased to inform you that this evidence solidly substantiates the FLCCC's recommendation that Ivermectin should be adopted globally and systematically for the prevention and treatment of COVID-19. Because I know there is a lot of fake news going about, I would like to assure you that you can trust the integrity of my report because I am an experienced independent medical research consultant whose work is routinely used to underpin international clinical practice guidelines. In addition, I have no conflict of interest and have received no funding for this report."

Dr. Marc Wathelet, a Harvard-trained virologist, also reviewed the current failing efforts to contain the pandemic. He summed up the problem and his solution, "The selective pressure of the antibodies (from vaccines) will select viruses that are able to escape the antibodies – so that's a danger – and we already see that happening with the different mutants. So a great advantage of Ivermectin over vaccination is the fact the virus cannot evolve resistance to it."

The bottom line is scientific humility, something that is required in public health leadership. Dr. Peter McCullough warns that, "We have to have a lot of humility." When we realize that variant strains are emerging that overcome our mass vaccination policy, the answer is not more booster shots and more lockdowns. When what we are doing is not working, we must have the scientific humility to get another independent scientific opinion and change our approach.

The answer does not have to be abandoning vaccination; it can be simply adding sequential drugs and nutraceuticals as Dr. George Fareed and Dr. Peter McCullough have published extensively here https://rcm.imrpress.com/EN/10.31083/j.rcm.2020.04.264 .

Dr. Fareed has further refined his combination of sequential drugs and nutraceuticals to include both antivirals, HCQ and Ivermectin as they complement each other. He notes that they can work synergistically as they have different mechanisms of action. Dr. Fareed has also added other medications including steroids, anticoagulants, colchicine, and fluvoxamine based upon newer scientific studies.

Another virologist, Dr. Wathelet, provided further input. He had researched the first SARS virus extensively more than a decade before the pandemic began. He is one of the few true experts on the SARS and coronaviruses. He warned the Belgium government as early as February of 2020 about the consequences of the current pandemic. And he was correct. Dr. Wathelet now proposes that Ivermectin be given to all those infected and all their contacts. He notes it would crush the pandemic in a matter of weeks. "Just a few weeks is all it would take. What are we waiting for?"

Dr. Pierre Kory observes that Bangladesh has effectively already done this. They have been using Ivermectin since November and giving it to all those infected and all their contacts: "They were predicted to have two million deaths based upon the size and density of their population. They were thought to be decimated. They adopted Ivermectin very early on. There are newspaper reports that every household takes Ivermectin."

In a country of 160 million people, they now have only 8,000 deaths. In our country of twice that population, we now have 547,000 deaths, more than 68 times as many. Dr. Kory maintains that no more studies are required to make the decision to use Ivermectin.

"The data is unassailable when you see the mountains, the totality and the breadth of the data. It's really hard to take (the failure of our regulators to use Ivermectin to save lives)."

Dr. Tess Lawrie wrote an Open Letter to Prime Minister Boris Johnson on January 9, 2021, pleading for him to implement Ivermectin, "But most of all you can trust me because I am a medical doctor first and foremost with a moral duty to help people, to do no harm and to save lives. Please may we start saving lives now."

She has received no reply to date.

Until our regulatory agencies decide to implement Ivermectin, or even approve its use, most of us are left with no recourse except for attorneys like Ralph Lorigo and Bongani Luthuli to fight for our health care rights.

We will be left with those outspoken experts like Dr. Peter McCullough, Dr. George Fareed, Dr. Pierre Kory, Dr. Tess Lawrie, and Dr. Marc Wathelet to enlighten our leaders. We are counting on you, the reader, to insist our leaders listen to them – and change our current health policies.

Write your Senators or Congressmen. Notify your President or Prime Minister. Sign the petition below. In the words of Dr. Tess Lawrie – Please may we start saving lives now?

Help Support Dr. Lawrie's Non-Profit Effort

Please support Dr. Tess Lawrie's magnificent effort. She has begun a non-profit corporation to accelerate global approval of Ivermectin to save lives. Visit her gofundme website and video:

https://vimeo.com/531195548

Chapter 7

COURT BATTLES GIVE RISE TO DAVID V. GOLIATH SHOWDOWN

It was bad enough that Dr. Andrew Hill had discovered Ivermectin was life-saving by conducting his own meta-analysis. For those readers not familiar with the term "meta-analysis," it refers to a pooling of the data.

For instance, if one has 15 studies that point to a drug's effectiveness and four that show a null or negative effect, someone like Dr. Hill can combine these into one large data set and get an overall result. This often proves more helpful than trying to make sense of individual results. When Dr. Hill did this with the dozens of Ivermectin studies, he found a profoundly positive effect, so positive that he excitedly pre-announced his results in an interview, much to the chagrin of his financial sponsors.

https://youtu.be/yOAh7GtvcOs

However, he was reigned in before more damage was done. First, he was invited to the NIH, along with Dr. Marik, probably to give the appearance of propriety. Second, he was given a gag order and told to not speak to any more press until the WHO made an official decision on Ivermectin. It turned out that this decision would go against the drug despite Dr. Hill's findings. Finally, Dr. Hill's conclusion would be changed by someone else, and the rest is history.

However, containing Dr. Hill would prove far simpler than containing Dr. Tess Lawrie, who did her own meta-analysis, and came to the same conclusions as Dr. Hill and Dr. Kory before her. She found overwhelming evidence of Ivermectin's profound ability to reduce death in all stages of COVID-19. Naturally, she did what any good and ethical doctor would do in her shoes. She alerted the health minister and Prime Minister Boris Johnson by written letter and by video. Please review her following video letter to Boris Johnson in early January imploring him to act to implement the drug immediately:

https://youtu.be/M8RMBa1UfsE

Predictably, her letter was ignored. But the damage had been done. Once again, the wagons were circled. The new study from Colombia was published in the prestigious JAMA, where Ivermectin was said to show no effect in a group of young South Americans. This was particularly curious to many, and the major journals had given Ivermectin the silent treatment previously, yet now were suddenly taking an interest in an obscure study by an obscure researcher. However, this researcher had received funding from Johnson and Johnson and Merck. The study was roundly criticized as flawed by a group of 120 physicians who wrote an open letter.

Dr. Tess Lawrie was so frustrated she launched a non-profit corporation to get Ivermectin approved through a gofundme campaign. This author attempted to start a change.org petition that was first ignored but taken down after it garnered some 1300 signatures. These feeble attempts to battle Big Pharma and Big Regulators paled compared to the countermeasures and brought up comparisons with David and Goliath. I continued with my "Letter to the Editor" campaign. They could not silence The Desert Review. Thank God.

Open Letter to Boris Johnson from Tess Lawrie

Originally published March 10, 2021

Dr. Tess Lawrie, Consultant to the WHO

Dr. Tess Lawrie is the Director of Evidenced Based Medicine Consultancy in Bath, UK. Her work is routinely relied upon to underpin international medical practice guidelines. She has no conflicts of interest.

She now joins the growing ranks of international physicians that have penned "open letters" to national officials to use early outpatient treatment with repurposed drugs to save lives in this great pandemic.

Dr. George Fareed began the movement on August 11, 2020 when he wrote an Open Letter to Dr. Anthony Fauci, the Director of the NIAH. This was followed by Dr. Naseeba Kathrada who wrote an Open Letter to South African President Cyril Ramaphosa. Now we see Dr. Tess Lawrie's Open Letter to U.K. Prime Minister Boris Johnson.

Dr. Lawrie compiled the results of her meta-analysis of 27 studies showing Ivermectin's effectiveness at saving lives and submitted them to the U.K's Health Secretary Hancock on January 3rd. No reply. This was similar to Dr. Fareed's experience. His letter launched a Congressional Inquiry and two Senate Hearings. Additionally the Senate delivered a condensed version of Fareed's letter to Dr. Anthony Fauci via the Senate Liaison to the NIH. No answer yet either.

Dr. Fareed's full letter is published in my book, "Surviving Cancer, COVID-19 & Disease: The Repurposed Drug Revolution.

Dr. Tess Lawrie's letter is published below, along with her video to the Prime Minister. It seems Boris Johnson is not as concerned with saving lives as Dr. Lawrie. Perhaps it is because he is a politician, and must be careful not to offend certain powerful interests. However Dr. Fauci is a physician and is thus bound by the Hippocratic oath.

All physicians, Dr. Lawrie points out are bound by the Helsinki Declaration which states that the "wellbeing of the patient should take precedence over the interests of science and society." Dr. Lawrie says that means that since the data conclusively already demonstrate the life-saving benefits of Ivermectin, that to give a control group of patients a placebo would violate this ethic. Her letter and video are presented below.

After you review this, please urge your Senators and Congressman and other elected officials to take action and pressure your state and national representatives to ask Dr. Fauci what he is waiting for. Meanwhile I update the Kory Count, the number of preventable deaths that have occurred since the Senate Testimony made clear that early outpatient treatment was scientifically proven and available.

Dr. Tess Lawrie's Letter to Boris Johnson dated January 9, 2021:

"The good news is that we now have solid evidence of an effective treatment Covid-19. It is called ivermectin. Ivermectin is a very safe and effective anti-parasitic medication widely used in low and middle income countries to treat worms, lice and scabies in both adults and children. It has been around for decades and not only is it on the WHO list of essential medicines it is a Nobel Prize winning medicine due to its increasing usefulness across a range of illnesses.

Between Xmas and new year I independently reviewed 27 studies presented by the FLCCC as evidence of ivermectin effectiveness. The resulting evidence is consistent and unequivocal : ivermectin works well

both in preventing covid infections and in preventing deaths at the same doses used to treat lice other parasitic infections.

I am very pleased to inform you that this evidence solidly substantiates the FLCCC's recommendation that ivermectin should be adopted globally and systematically for the prevention and treatment of Covid-19.

Because I know there is alot of fake news going about I would like to assure you that you can trust the integrity of my report because I am an experienced independent medical research consultant whose work is routinely used to underpin international clinical practice guidelines. In addition I have no conflict of interest and have received no funding for this report.

But most of all you can trust me because I am a medical doctor first and foremost with a moral duty to help people, to do no harm and to save lives.

https://youtu.be/M8RMBa1UfsE

The Kory Count is now, sadly updated. I keep the Kory Count out of respect for the dead, in remembering that most of these lives could have been saved if early outpatient treatment with repurposed drugs had been adopted by our country's health policy makers when they were first made aware, with the first Senate Hearing of November 18, 2020 with the testimony of distinguished experts, Dr. Peter McCollough, Dr. George Fareed, and Dr. Harvey Risch.

Beginning Kory Count as of February 1, 2021: 190,893 lives

02/02/21: 3611.	02/11/21: 3878.	02/20/21: 1831
02/03/21: 3843.	02/12/21: 5463.	02/21/21: 1247
02/04/21: 5117.	02/13/21: 3373.	02/22/21: 1454
02/05/21: 3570.	02/14/21: 1080.	02/23/21: 2328
02/06/21: 2662.	02/15/21: 994.	02/24/21: 3210
02/07/21: 1301.	02/16/21: 1707.	02/25/21: 2465
02/08/21: 1583.	02/17/21: 2471.	02/26/21: 2176
02/09/21: 3170.	02/18/21: 2625.	02/27/21: 1567
02/10/21: 3254.	02/19/21: 2621.	02/28/21: 1129

03/01/21: 1425
03/02/21: 1306
03/03/21: 2369
03/04/21: 1949
03/05/21: 2483
03/06/21: 1459
03/07/21: 682
03/08/21: 815
03/09/21: 1885

The Kory Count: Total Preventable COVID-19 Deaths through 03/09/21: 274,996

300,000 Preventable COVID Deaths: A Sad Reflection

*Originally published by The Desert Review
April 2, 2021*

History Will Judge

Our great nation, the United States, for all its ideals, has not enacted a public health policy of early outpatient treatment for COVID-19. Despite compelling evidence that repurposed drugs can and do prevent deaths, there is no FDA or NIH guidance to the public or physicians to offer patients anything else except vaccines and ventilators, masks and lockdowns.

Our sad official policy is to sicken at home. If one turns blue or cannot breathe, the FDA policy is to only then enter the hospital. No specific drug treatment is advised at home despite the November 19, 2020, Senate Testimony of Dr. Peter McCullough, Dr. Harvey Risch, and Dr. George Fareed, all who advised early outpatient treatment with triple therapy of an antiviral, an antibiotic, and Zinc. At that point, deaths in our nation were only at about 250,000. Today they stand at nearly 560,000.

"History will not look kindly at us," says Dr. Peter McCullough. When all is said and done, and future generations ask, "Really, you did not offer to treat them?" - Because the government said not to do so. And you were aware of the data on Ivermectin? And Vitamin D, and Hydroxychloroquine?
You saw that 27 randomized controlled studies all showed a mortality reduction of large magnitude. You saw that there was at least a 68% reduction in death with Ivermectin use - and you failed to recommend or even inform patients?

Yes. This period will go down in history as one of the darkest episodes for physicians.
We cannot defend it - We cannot explain it - And we cannot escape it. On December 13, 2020, just fine days after Dr. Pierre Kory's passionate testimony delivered to the US Senate, I coined the term, Kory Count.

The Kory Count was begun to memorialize permanently the needless deaths resulting from a failure in public health policy, those deaths that could have been prevented, if only the testimony by expert physicians had been heeded.

Dr. Pierre Kory stated that any deaths then (as of December 8, 2020), knowing that early outpatient treatment is life-saving, are preventable. The Kory Count is the running tally of the number of COVID-19 deaths that could have been prevented using such early outpatient treatment. Dr. Peter McCullough asked the FDA to approve Early Outpatient Treatment on November 19, 2020 - including the use of Ivermectin.

Court Battles Give Rise to David v. Goliath Showdown

So today on April 1, 2021, I update the Kory Count.

It is out of reverence to the dead, those people whose lives could have been saved had early outpatient treatment become the health care policy of the land on November 19, 2020.
Dennis Prager has said to doctors collectively, "Shame on you." For physicians everywhere to know the truth, to know the results of numerous meta-analyses now completed by Dr. Tess Lawrie, Dr. Andrew Hill, and Dr. Pierre Kory on Ivermectin - and to know that deaths are reduced dramatically when this is used early and even late in the disease - and to not offer it to all high-risk patients, is unethical and contrary to our Hippocratic oath.

The reasons the WHO and FDA have rejected Ivermectin have nothing to do with science, and everything to do with corruption by Big Pharma.

I now update the Kory Count as it closes in on 300,000 preventable deaths:

Beginning Kory Count as of 03/09/21: 274,996

- 03/10/21: 1447
- 03/11/21: 1522
- 03/12/21: 1757
- 03/13/21: 1846
- 03/14/21: 572
- 03/15/21: 751
- 03/16/21: 1245
- 03/17/21: 1177
- 03/18/21: 1558
- 03/19/21: 1513
- 03/20/21: 773

- 03/21/21: 444
- 03/22/21: 650
- 03/23/21: 892
- 03/24/21: 1591
- 03/25/21: 1270
- 03/26/21: 1260
- 03/27/21: 780
- 03/29/21: 685
- 03/30/21: 948
- 03/31/21: 1138

- 03/31/21 KORY COUNT: 299,252

SAVE COVID LIVES:
Dr. Tess Lawrie Rallies the World

Originally Published April 9, 2021

SAVECOVIDLIVES:
The Link that was Taken Down: Why?

Dr. Tess Lawrie has emerged as the new face of the Ivermectin Movement. Her involvement began in January after she reported the results of her meta-analysis to Boris Johnson and the National Health Service.

After performing a detailed synthesis of dozens of studies, her conclusions agreed with those of others, including the FLCCC, that Ivermectin should be adopted globally and systematically for the treatment of COVID-19. Due to the urgency of the matter, she drafted a letter to Prime Minister Johnson which was underscored with this video:

https://vimeo.com/513332647

When it became apparent that her recommendations were being ignored, she redoubled her efforts and decided to begin a new organization designed to help Ivermectin get approved by national and international regulatory bodies.

In the United States, a number of physicians have advocated for early outpatient treatment through various scholarly publications and by speaking to the US Senate Committee on Homeland Security, culminating with Dr. Pierre Kory's powerful appeal made on December 8, 2020.

The video of Dr. Kory's speech went viral before it was famously censored by YouTube, which actually drew more attention to the cause. Subsequently, patients across the United States have asked for, and in some cases demanded Ivermectin. Hospitalized patients have been routinely denied the drug, and this has created lawsuits and highly publicized cases of recovery with Ivermectin following court orders for the hospital to administer it.

Despite the science, and the remarkable cases of success, the US and UK agencies have refused to approve Ivermectin. The W.H.O. ruled against recommending Ivermectin despite their report showing an average 81% reduction in death associated with Ivermectin usage. Dr. Lawrie has tried to make sense of the W.H.O. report which appeared contradictory, flawed, and inaccurate.

https://youtu.be/D2ju5v4TAaQ

Convinced that Ivermectin has been railroaded due to "investment in novel therapies," Dr. Lawrie has taken up the Ivermectin torch to save lives in the COVID pandemic. She discusses the reasons behind starting her new company to get Ivermectin approved.

Court Battles Give Rise to David v. Goliath Showdown

https://vimeo.com/531195548

Dr. Lawrie heads the BIRD panel, The British Ivermectin Development panel of distinguished world scientists who reported to the W.H.O. As the Pandemic threatens a fourth wave, and at least a half a dozen new variants, it is becoming obvious that a Vaccine-only policy may not be the answer. Scientists and practicing physicians are calling for the approval of Ivermectin in all major countries of the world. South Africa has set a legal precedent by taking their government's regulatory agency, SAHPRA, to court, and winning.

Tess Lawrie is now rallying the world to get this cheap, repurposed and Nobel Prize Winning drug approved, and many believe this addition will be necessary to resolve the Pandemic.

https://rumble.com/embed/vcuq4b/?pub=4

Our Petition on change.org is entitled "Provide Access and Information on Ivermectin; Help us get a life-saving drug approved" is gaining momentum. The petition is addressed to UK Prime Minister Boris Johnson, US President Joe Biden, and the NIH, FDA, CDC, WHO, and the NHS.

https://www.change.org/SaveCovidLives

Editors's Note: The above referenced change.org petition acquired 1270 signatures over the ensuing three weeks. As support for the petition from overseas and the US accelerated, some powerful interests stepped in, and on April 10, 2021 the movement became too much to bear for the opposition.

There was mass censorship of multiple sites at the same time. The following article struck a nerve with some well-financed and well-connected entity.

The article published in both *The Economic Standard* and *The Desert Review* on April 10, 2021 and within hours of its debut, the article was taken down by The Economic Standard "under protest" and a gag order.

Within the same time, on the same date, the change.org petition www.change.org//savecovidlives was also taken down.

Two days after the following article's publication Merck, the seventh largest pharmaceutical corporation in the world, announced it was abandoning development of MK-7110 for COVID, something that had been exposed in the article. *The Desert Review*, however, could not be swayed, and the article remains proudly posted there for your review today.

https://www.thedesertreview.com/opinion/letters_to_editor/big-pharma-uses-big-tobaccos-strategy-to-defeat-ivermectin/article_fc17022e-9ba6-11eb-8c7b-633764c1bf9e.html

Without further delay, I now present this controversial article:

Big Pharma Uses Big Tobacco's Strategy to Defeat Ivermectin

Originally published by The Economic Standard and The Desert Review on April 10, 2021

In the 1950's scientists Richard Doll and Bradford Hill published a study from the UK finding that the risk of lung cancer was related to the number of cigarettes smoked per day, and this risk was 25 times higher in those who smoked more than 25 cigarettes per day.

Other scientists, namely Ernest Wynder and Evarts Graham, found a strong association between bronchogenic carcinoma and smoking. 96.5% of men with bronchogenic carcinoma were heavy chain smokers compared to 73.7% of the general population. Several extensive studies within one year of each other found the same thing, cigarette smoking is strongly related to lung cancer, and the more one smoked, the higher one's risk.

The big problem was that the cigarette industry was a multibillion-dollar lobby by the mid- 1960s. And they were not about to allow a few renegade scientists to spoil their profits. The Marlboro Man, as Dr. Mukherjee wrote in his Pulitzer Prize-winning book, *The Emperor of All Maladies*, was the most successful smoking icon by 1955. Dr. Mukherjee describes how the Tobacco Industry fought back by twisting science against the public, first by arguing that an association does not prove cause and effect, and later by offering to perform the studies.

The tobacco scientists argued that lung cancer was caused by genetics: if you were born with cancer genes, you developed cancer, and if you weren't, you didn't get it. Cigarettes might be associated with cancer, but they argued that more studies were needed if one were to actually "prove a causal link" between cigarettes and cancer. The actual cause of lung cancer, the tobacco scientists concluded, was faulty genetics and not cigarettes.

To assist with these studies, the generous Big Tobacco Industry even offered to fund the research by founding the Tobacco Industry Research Committee. The TIRC is described further in *The Emperor of All Maladies*, a book I strongly recommend everyone read. The author writes how this ingenious strategy kept the tobacco companies in business and record-breaking profits for the next 50 years despite causing many millions of lung cancer deaths.

Blurring or confusing the facts as a tactic proved remarkably effective. But by far, the craftiest ruse was for Big Tobacco to pretend to embrace the research and set up their own studies. Because by controlling the study design, they could control the outcome.

The same strategy is now used against the public in this pandemic.

Their first victim was Hydroxychloroquine, which proved easy to discredit given that Donald Trump sounded unhinged in his praise for the drug. Later studies seemed to reinforce the belief that HCQ was ineffective; however when academic misconduct was found, it threatened to expose the effort. Big Pharma successfully distanced itself when the fraudulent articles were retracted and blamed on lone scientists acting by themselves.

Dr. Tess Lawrie is a highly-respected and independent research consultant to the World Health Organization and NHS. Her work is routinely relied upon in the formation of International Practice Guidelines. She has found HCQ to have an effect against the coronavirus. Most tellingly, when Dr. Tess Lawrie performed her independent review of the data on Ivermectin, she removed the Fonseca study, which purported to show no benefit against COVID with Ivermectin use.

Dr. Lawrie explained, "They (The Fonseca Group) didn't find that much of a difference between Ivermectin and the control arm. But the control arm received HCQ. So basically, there's a comparison between two fairly active treatments." Dr. Lawrie explained that there were many reasons to consider HCQ active against the virus. Thus, two patient groups were compared in Fonseca, both of which received effective drugs against COVID-19, and this was not considered a valid controlled trial of Ivermectin. Therefore the study was eliminated from the meta-analysis.
https://youtu.be/D2ju5v4TAaQ

Doctors across the nation continue to employ both drugs in an antiviral cocktail comprised of HCQ, Ivermectin, Zinc and Vitamin D. In particular, former Harvard professor and NIH researcher Dr. George Fareed of the Imperial Valley has published on this approach and enjoyed remarkable success.

https://www.thedesertreview.com/health/local-frontline-doctors-modify-covid-treatment-based-on-results/article_9cdded9e-962f-11eb-a59a-f3e1151e98c3.html

He and his associate, Dr. Brian Tyson, have treated over 5,000 COVID-19 patients with only two deaths. Dr. Fareed pioneered the first HIV clinic in Brawley, California, and notes that the cocktail approach was necessary and became the standard of care in such conditions as HIV and HCV. He feels it is also essential with COVID-19.

Today we know that the earlier Ivermectin is given, the lower the death rate. We learned in the 1950s that the more cigarettes one smoked, and the longer they smoked, the higher the death rate. We now have 50 studies all showing Ivermectin's benefits across all stages of COVID-19, with The World Health Organization finding an average of 81% decreased mortality.

Merck and the FDA came out against Ivermectin only after the US government contributed 356 million dollars to Merck to develop MK-7110, an anti-COVID drug. This occurred after Merck purchased the rights to MK-7110 for 425 million dollars in a deal announced on December 23, 2020. The chances of this drug receiving approval by the FDA are very high.

The chances of Ivermectin successfully competing against MK-7110, if Ivermectin is also approved, are also high. It is, therefore, logical that a multi-billion dollar industry will use its immense lobbying, media, and advertising power to prevent this.

The smoking gun here is that Merck was the original developer of Ivermectin, but now that their old drug is generic and no longer profitable, it is being tossed under the proverbial bus.

Obfuscation and the "offer-to-fund-the-research" through a time-honored and proven strategy of manipulation is once again proving remarkably effective in swaying public opinion.

We have seen this movie before with Big Tobacco.

We already know how it ends. We have 50 studies, all showing Ivermectin's life-saving benefits. We do not need 50 more to tell that Ivermectin prevents COVID death and should be adopted immediately.

The science is clear based upon numerous meta-analyses already performed by world-class and respected scientists Dr. Tess Lawrie, Dr. Andrew Hill, and Dr. Pierre Kory.
This brings me to the *Washington Post's* April 8, 2021 article which announced that the government planned to do their own Ivermectin study. Thanks, but no thanks, to the NIH, in their magnanimous offer to conduct more "research." We already know what they will find.

Editor's Note: Merck's 356 million dollar deal with the US government was exposed in this article published on April 10, 2021. On April 15 Merck reacted, and announced they were discontinuing plans to develop MK-7110 for COVID-19 with the following press release on Business Wire,

"Merck has determined to discontinue development of MK-7110 for COVID-19 and to focus its pandemic efforts on advancing molnupiravir and on producing Johnson & Johnson's COVID-19 vaccine."

https://www.businesswire.com/news/home/20210415005251/en/Merck-to-Discontinue-Development-of-MK-7110-for-COVID-19

Thomas Jefferson Weighs In

The link between Big Pharma and Big Regulators has never been clearer. Thomas Jefferson, a founding father of the United States, and co-author of the Declaration of Independence feared precisely this type of situation.

He feared that at some point in the future, a governmental authority might use a pretense, a guise, to confiscate our personal human rights, our freedoms to travel (vaccine passport), to assemble (shelter in place), to work (mandatory quarantines and closures of non-essential businesses), to speak (mass censorship about Ivermectin), to choose medical care (Ivermectin), to refuse medical care (vaccines) in the name of public safety (pandemic):

> *"There is no justification for taking away individual freedom in the guise of public safety."*
>
> -Thomas Jefferson

Provide Access and Information on Ivermectin: Change.org

Originally published April 10, 2021

Censorship took this petition down today. It is obvious who did it.

For all who supported this petition, please read the following article because within hours of its publication this petition [after three weeks of no issues] was abruptly and summarily taken down.This is the writing that triggered this reaction:

https://www.thedesertreview.com/opinion/letters_to_editor/big-pharma-uses-big-tobaccos-strategy-to-defeat-ivermectin/article_fc17022e-9ba6-11eb-8c7b-633764c1bf9e.html?utm_medium=social&utm_source=email&utm_campaign=user-share

I will leave it to the reader to conclude who is responsible for censorship of this change.org petition. This petition was started on Change.org on 03/21/21 and the official link was:

https://change.org/savecovidlives

The original name of the Petition was: **"Provide Access and Information on Ivermectin: Stop the COVID-19 Deaths Now."** The name was changed in April to **"Provide Access and Information on Ivermectin: Help Us Get A Life-Saving Drug Approved for COVID-19."**

Ivermectin for the World

The Petition was addressed to: *Dr. Anthony Fauci (NIAID), Joseph Biden (President), Dr. Francis Collins (NIH), Dr. Janet Woodcock (FDA), Dr. Tedros Adhanom Ghebreyesus (WHO), Dr. Stephen Powis (NHS).*

The petition drew widespread world-wide support and garnered more than 1270 signatures from celebrities, scientists, inventors, radio and television commentators, and most importantly, from practicing physicians.

We received comments in favor of this petition from as far away as South Africa, Ireland, Australia, Canada, Slovakia and the UK. People all over the globe expressed support for the petition as well as outrage toward those who would oppose access to a life-saving drug.

Please redouble your efforts to support Ivermectin by supporting Dr. Tess Lawrie and her work:
https://vimeo.com/531195548

Please redouble your efforts to support Ivermectin by supporting Dr. Pierre Kory and the FLCCC. www.covid19criticalcare.com

Please support the work of Dr. Peter McCullough, Dr. George Fareed and Dr. Harvey Risch as well as the American Association of Physicians & Surgeons.

https://rcm.imrpress.com/EN/10.31083/j.rcm.2020.04.264

Please share the following free brochure with all your friends and family and social media:
https://aapsonline.org/CovidPatientTreatmentGuide.pdf

We will get the word out.

Truth has a way of finding it's audience.

Ivermectin Wins in Court Again: For Human Rights

Originally published in The Desert Review on April 21, 2021

One dose of Ivermectin was all it took to get 81-year-old John Swanson off the ventilator. John's wife Sandra could not believe it. His story is remarkably similar to other cases of patients who were on their way out with advanced COVID-19 but saved when Ivermectin was added.

Ralph Lorigo is the lawyer who now has won three court orders forcing New York hospitals to administer Ivermectin to dying patients. Incredibly, these three hospitals and their lawyers fought against the patients, arguing they did not have the right to receive the drug despite a valid prescription written by their doctors. In essence, the argument was that they did not have the right to try a potentially life-saving medication.

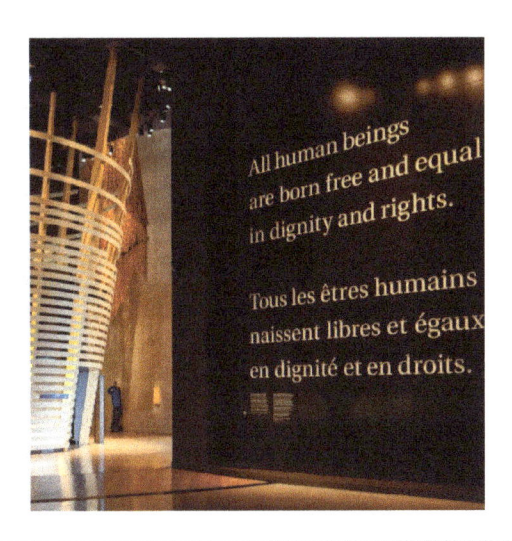

In each of the three cases, the New York State Supreme Court Justices sided with the patient, and in each of the three cases, the patients made near-miraculous recoveries after the Ivermectin was given. In each case, these patients were in the Intensive Care Unit on ventilators, unable to breathe on their own, and universally, after the drug was given, they rapidly improved and were able to breathe on their own.

Judith Smentkiewicz made national news in January when her family hired Lorigo after the hospital refused a fourth dose of Ivermectin. Smentkiewicz's son and daughter called Ivermectin a "miracle drug" in court papers. Attorney Lorigo and his associate, Jon F. Minear, reported, "This lady was on a ventilator, literally on her deathbed, before she was given this drug. As far as we're concerned, the judge's order saved this woman's life."

The family of Glenna "Sue" Dickinson happened to see a newspaper article of Judith's remarkable story, and they decided to try Ivermectin as well.

Sue Dickinson, 65, contracted COVID-19 on Jan. 7, 2021. She suffered progressive worsening and was admitted to Rochester General Hospital on Jan. 12. She continued to worsen and was placed on a ventilator on Jan. 17. The hospital staff advised that her chances of survival were about 40%.

With nothing to lose, Natalie Kingdollar, Dickinson's daughter, reached out to their family doctor, Tom Madejski, who wrote the prescription. The hospital refused to give Sue the Ivermectin. The legal team of Lorigo and Minear drafted an affidavit from Dr. Madejski and sought an injunction. State Supreme Court Justice Frank Caruso ordered the hospital to provide the Ivermectin.

Dickinson, like Swanson, and Smentkiewicz, came off the ventilator and improved as well. The family reported on Facebook that, "She's making progress each day, and it's Ivermectin and God making this happen." She has since been released from the hospital.

Ivermectin is widely used by physicians, as there are now 51 studies from around the world, with 50 showing clear benefit and one showing neutral. However, the lone study showing a neutral effect was roundly criticized as flawed in an open letter signed by a group of 120 physicians.

https://trialsitenews.com/open-letter-by-u-s-doctors-jama-ivermectin-study-is-fatally-flawed/

Experts worldwide have called for the global and systematic use of Ivermectin to prevent and treat COVID-19. Physicians have recently written about a profit motive by regulatory agencies and Big Pharma to block cheap, safe, and effective treatments like Ivermectin and HCQ in favor of experimental and perhaps more dangerous and arguably less effective vaccines and medicines like Remdesivir. With Remdesivir costing 3,100 dollars per dose and not reducing deaths, the choice of Ivermectin is a no-brainer say many doctors.

Ivermectin costs about two dollars per dose. It is safer than Tylenol or most vitamins, says Dr. Pierre Kory of the FLCCC Alliance, a group of expert physicians promoting access and information through a non-profit organization. Dr. Kory and Mr. Lorigo have teamed up to help other hospitalized patients gain access to the life-saving drug.

Dr. Fred Wagshul, a Yale-educated physician, is a Pulmonary specialist and directs the Lung Center of America. He is also a founding member of the FLCCC Alliance. Dr. Wagshul notes that the typical dose for hospitalized patients is 0.3 mg of Ivermectin per kg of body weight for four days which works out to nine 3 mg tablets daily for four days in a typical 200-pound patient.

Dr. George Fareed, former Harvard professor, advocates combination therapy of Ivermectin with HCQ in outpatient cases. For the benefit of physician readers, the specific doses are provided in this link:

https://www.thedesertreview.com/health/local-frontline-doctors-modify-covid-treatment-based-on-results/article_9cdded9e-962f-11eb-a59a-f3e1151e98c3.html

The big problem is that information promoting Ivermectin is often censored or silenced as quickly as it is provided. Facebook, Reddit, Change.org, YouTube, and others have recently taken down posts on Ivermectin citing violation of "community standards."

Physicians who employ good judgment and scientific studies are considered violators, as well as those who publish factual accounts of Ivermectin-based recovery stories. A recent article exposed the link between large pharmaceutical corporations and government regulatory agencies who have financial entanglements and massive conflicts of interest:

https://www.thedesertreview.com/opinion/letters_to_editor/big-pharma-uses-big-tobaccos-strategy-to-defeat-ivermectin/article_fc17022e-9ba6-11eb-8c7b-633764c1bf9e.html

The disinformation campaign is evident with the publication of articles attempting to cast Ivermectin in a false light, referring to it as an "animal dewormer" that might be a "bad idea" for humans to use. In reality, many drugs are common to both humans and animals for treatment, including antibiotics, antifungals, and antiparasitic agents.

Ampicillin, a form of penicillin, has been widely used to treat infections in children like whooping cough, salmonella, and meningitis. It has been routinely used to treat adults for bronchitis, pneumonia, and rheumatic heart disease. It is also consistently employed in veterinary applications to treat calves, cattle, dogs and cats.

You would never see an article attempting to smear Ampicillin as an animal drug and warn people against taking it. However, we see this propaganda daily trying to influence the general public against Ivermectin, a life-saving drug that has been prescribed safely and in billions of doses over the past 40 years for parasitic disease.

Dr. Satoshi Omura won the 2015 Nobel Prize in Medicine for his discoveries leading to the development of Ivermectin. In his praise for Ivermectin and its potential to help in the COVID-19 pandemic, Dr. Omura recently compared Ivermectin to Penicillin, "one of the greatest discoveries of the twentieth century."

http://jja-contents.wdc-jp.com/pdf/JJA74/74-1-open/74-1_44-95.pdf

Currently, Ivermectin has already been adopted by 25% of the world's countries to prevent and treat COVID-19. Bangladesh, where Ivermectin is broadly used in almost every home, enjoys a 99% lower per capita death rate from COVID-19 than the US. Bangladesh, with 160 million inhabitants, has half the US population. However, it has merely 10,000 COVID-19 deaths.

Contrast that with nearly 580,000 US deaths in our country of 327 million.

However, censorship, corruption, hospital lawyers, and disinformation campaigns have continued to stand in the way of its widespread acceptance in the United States. Many have never even heard of it.

Ivermectin recently won in court in South Africa after a protracted legal battle. Ralph Lorigo has now won his third State Supreme Court Injunction in New York. Will legal strategies also be required in the US to gain FDA approval for Ivermectin to treat COVID-19?

Dr. Tess Lawrie has entered this David v. Goliath battle. She is an independent research consultant to the WHO, and her work has consistently been used to underpin International Clinic Practice Guidelines. In other words, she has been one of the go-to scientists on which the WHO bases their recommendations.

She has established a non-profit organization to promote the worldwide approval and adoption of Ivermectin for COVID-19. She is requesting support through this video:

https://vimeo.com/531195548

We owe it to ourselves as human beings to support this work. We owe it to future generations who need medical truth, not corruption, to guide our public health policy. We owe it to the principle of basic human rights.

India's Humanitarian Crisis

This brings us to the end of our Ivermectin case. You are the judge and jury. You decide what action must be taken, immediately, before we lose any more lives. All these deaths going forward are preventable now that you have been made aware. Please feel the moral obligation to intervene. Recognize the awesome responsibility and opportunity we now all share to our fellow human beings.

Dr. Pierre Kory recently stated that the problem is no longer an issue with the science of repurposed drugs. With 52 studies completed involving some 17,500 patients and all except one (the flawed JAMA study that was objected to by 120 physicians) showing benefit, the science is not in question. Ivermectin is safe. Ivermectin is highly effective against all stages of COVID-19 in preventing death. The following link reporting the Ivermectin study data is updated daily. Please refer to it yourself (if they have not yet taken it down):

c19ivermectin.com

Dr. Kory explains the only remaining obstacle is Ivermectin suppression by powerful economic interests. He points the finger at the WHO, which receives funding with "strings attached." Most of the money they receive is conditioned on supporting the donors' wishes. And often, this means supporting vaccines and opposing repurposed drugs.

I now shift my focus to you, the reader. We, the concerned physicians, require your help to get the word out on Ivermectin to save lives. The great concern now is India.

India has enjoyed a low per capita infection rate of less than 1/10 that of the developed North American and European countries. Many reasons have been suggested, and were covered extensively in my last book on the Repurposed Drug Revolution, not the least of which included the widespread use of HCQ for malaria which is endemic to their continent. However, recently with the rise of more infectious variants including the Indian double mutant and South African strains, their cases and death rates have skyrocketed.

Their graph has gone exponential with no sign of slowing. Vaccination rates in India are less than 10% for even one shot, and the population has not been social distancing. Beyond that, Ivermectin use in India has been discouraged by the officials and has only in the past few days been included as an optional "add-on" to mild outpatient disease. Dr. Kory spoke to a hospital owner in India who stated:

"I have discussed about your (Ivermectin) webinar with my government doctors. They said not to participate in webinars about drugs not endorsed by the WHO."

Ivermectin is not used in Indian hospitals, and it appears nowhere in the official Indian Guidelines for severe or moderate hospitalized COVID cases. Instead, the usual standby of $3,100 per-dose Remdesivir remains popular.

The country has a 30% positive testing rate meaning there is much more human fuel to consume before this surge can be expected to slow down.

Sadly the combination of all of these factors equates to a perfect storm of viral spread throughout India – a true humanitarian crisis – and as Dr. Paul Marik has said "of unmitigated proportions."

We physicians must show leadership. We owe it to our fellow human beings to act – and to act swiftly and effectively.

Indian parents and grandparents are suffocating in front of their children while they wait in front of overflowing emergency rooms. They are dying in Taxi cabs parked in front of the hospital. With hospitals running out of oxygen, Indians are paying up to two months salary on the black market to purchase an oxygen tank to buy themselves one more day of breath.

With Ivermectin being dirt cheap, mere pennies, let us ship them the Ivermectin. Let us provide them the access and the information contained in this book.

It is offered free of charge through the e-book version on Kindle.

Ivermectin as this book has shown convincingly, is often effective in a single dose, and can liberate the most advanced COVID-19 patient from the ventilator within hours. Just imagine how far one million doses of Ivermectin would go to saving the 2,800 lives lost in that country today alone. During the period of time I have spent writing today, Ivermectin could have salvaged 80% or precisely 2,240 lives.

These lives could be someone's mother like Judith Smentkiewicz, they could be someone's father like Herman van de Westhuizen, or they could be someone's grandfather like John Swanson.

You and I are in the unique position of being able to save hundreds of thousands of lives through our political action. It need not cost any of us a cent. But if everyone speaks out to make this a reality, it most certainly will happen. Elected officials will respond if we picket. They will respond if we protest. If we speak out. Anything but complacency will win the day.

George Floyd taught us that.

This involves every bit as sacred a right. This involves our coveted rights as human beings to access life-saving medical care, regardless of what anyone says. We have the right to reject or accept anything we put in our bodies, regardless of what an authoritarian regime tells us. We have the absolute right to live in a free society regardless of censorship and widespread propaganda.

The point is that we know that Ivermectin works. Anyone who has read this book can tell exactly why Ivermectin is not in widespread use, and it has nothing to do with science.

I now bring my case to all the Christians and compassionate citizens and ask that they join me and my fellow physicians in getting help to India. Although the forces of censorship and misinformation have had their day, today is our day to right this wrong. It is our day, for the people of the world to unite in a show of morality and solidarity for human dignity.

My only regret is that I was unable to complete this book in time to save the 300,000 American lives lost since November when it was well known to the regulators and scientific community through dual Senate testimonies.

India is on a trajectory that portends far higher numbers if we fail to act now. We are staring a potential million casualties in the face. These are almost all preventable deaths. Let us summon the compassion within each of us to rise to the occasion.

If everyone acts and does one small thing, we can accomplish the saving of India with Ivermectin. One hundred million Americans and Europeans all working together in a humanitarian effort can and will be effective.

I am reminded of a famous doctor, a member of a past generation who rallied soldiers to take up the fight after he passed away. He is best known as the poet physician who wrote the words to Flander's Fields. But he is also a casualty of the last great pandemic of our world, The Spanish Flu.

Please ponder his message as you rest in comfort with your family. Please consider what he meant with those verses in Flanders Fields. Please consider Dr. John McRae's prophetic words that were in part meant to signal you to action at this moment, and in this pandemic.

The torch is ours. The choice to protest, to ask our pastors to preach about India and Ivermectin, to demand justice from our Congressman, Senators, Governors, President or Prime Minister is up to each of us.

Demand that India be shipped oxygen tanks, demand that India be shipped dexamethasone, and demand most urgently that India be shipped millions of tablets of Ivermectin.

President Biden has the power to order Ivermectin's mass manufacture and distribution to provide humanitarian aide to India. Please insist that he do so.

Insist that it be given to all patients waiting in line at Indian hospitals. Provide free bottled water to drink down the medication.

Will we stand for human rights, and act to save India from COVID using Ivermectin, or we will fail? What would Dr. McRae say and do?

In the words of my fellow physician, Dr. Tess Lawrie, "May we please start saving lives now?"

Doctor John McCrae:
Spanish Flu Casualty; The Poem

Originally published September 1, 2020

Dr. John McRae, Physician, Soldier, and Poet

Court Battles Give Rise to David v. Goliath Showdown

John McCrae M.D. was a Spanish Flu Casualty. He developed pneumonia. This was caused by a zoonotic virus, one that comes from an animal.

Zoonotic viruses are notorious for causing pandemics and for stimulating the dreaded Cytokine Storm. Dr. John McCrae contracted a virus that turned into viral pneumonia, which spread to his brain, causing meningitis, ultimately ending the doctor's life.

His brother, Dr. Thomas McCrae, was a medical professor at the famed Johns Hopkins School of Medicine, and a close associate of the father of modern medicine, the great Sir William Osler.
John McCrae, on the other hand, studied medicine in Toronto, Canada.

He went into the Canadian military and rose to the rank of Lieutenant Colonel. He served as a surgeon during the Second Battle of Ypres in Belgium. He taught pathology at both the University of Vermont and McGill Medical Schools. He was an expert in infectious disease and was appointed as physician to the Alexandria Hospital for Contagious Diseases. Dr. McCrae, a learned physician, co-authored the medical textbook, A Textbook of Pathology for Students of Medicine.

But Dr. McCrae is not most remembered for being a fine and distinguished physician, although he was. He is not thought first and foremost a fine educator, although he was. He is not instantly renowned as a fine and courageous medical officer; however, heaven knows he was.

Dr. John McCrae, a victim of the Spanish Flu, remains forever known for the poem he penned in 1915.

Dr. McCrae crafted this poem the day after he lost his friend, Alex Helmer, to the Second Battle of Ypres in the

Flanders region of Belgium. The German army had cowardly used chlorine gas to kill human beings.

In 1915, more than a century ago, Dr. McRae wrote these words to inspire soldiers to rise up against the German army who had violated fundamental human rights using chemical weapons during the First World War.

Today in 2021, these verses ring as true as when he first penned them. But the threat is less obvious. Organizations we formerly trusted are now corrupt. Now we face far more dangerous adversaries, those treacherous opponents that would covertly rob us of our precious and inalienable rights to life and medical treatment. Let us all join John McRae in taking up the Flanders torch for the sake of humanity.

In Flanders Fields

-John McCrae MD, 1872-1918

"In Flanders fields the poppies blow
Between the crosses, row on row,
That mark our place; and in the sky
The larks, still bravely singing, fly
Scarce heard amid the guns below.

We are the Dead. Short days ago
We lived, felt dawn, saw sunset glow,
Loved and were loved, and now we lie
In Flanders fields.

Take up our quarrel with the foe:
To you from failing hands we throw
The torch; be yours to hold it high.
If ye break faith with us who die
We shall not sleep, though poppies grow
In Flanders fields."

Frequently Asked Questions

Q. I have heard the FDA and other opponents claim that although Ivermectin works against the coronavirus in the test tube, the dosage required to attain similar concentrations in humans would be toxic. Is that true?

A. No. That statement is based upon one cell culture experiment. It is a theory that has been disproven in dozens of randomized controlled trials showing Ivermectin's clinical effect at reducing death in thousands of patients around the world. The tissue levels obtained in these thousands of patients were sufficient to kill the virus, and they did not cause toxicity.

Q. Is it dangerous to take a horse or dog dewormer?

A. No one is suggesting anyone take a veterinary drug. However, many prescription medications are common to humans and animals, including antibiotics, analgesics, antivirals, and antiparasitic agents like Ivermectin. Animals are prescribed Ampicillin and ketoconazole, and Ivermectin. So are humans. Following your doctor's prescription for Ivermectin is both safe and effective. Never take your animal's medication.

Q. The FDA, European Medicines Agency, and the Infectious Disease Society of America all advise against taking Ivermectin for COVID-19. How can Ivermectin be truly effective if all these agencies advise against it?

A. The fact that the FDA, EMA, and IDSA advise against it does not mean Ivermectin does not work. Dr. Harvey Risch has said science is not based upon consensus. Only political parties are. Here we have all of these groups who are either directly or indirectly funded by the NIH. The NIH doles out 30 billion dollars a year, and those who speak out against the NIH's party line risk losing all or part of their funding.

Q. Almost everything I read or see on the internet or television says that Ivermectin is ineffective against COVID-19. If it works, why do I see mostly negative articles?

A. The media in general, gets payments from its advertisers. If you notice, the largest and wealthiest advertisers are no longer beer and cigarette companies. They are increasingly the pharmaceutical corporations advertising their newest prescription drugs. These advertisers can and do influence their media to obey their wishes regarding to keeping competing repurposed drugs in disfavor.

Q. You almost sound like a conspiracy theorist, right?

A. Not really. As a scientist, I do not subscribe to conspiracy theories. However, as a scientist, I remain guided by the data. And the scientific data are clear that Ivermectin has potent antiviral and anti-inflammatory activity, and it reduces deaths consistently and substantially in COVID-19.

Q. You sound like an anti-vaxxer, right?

A. No. I recommend that all my high-risk patients get vaccinated, so I am not an anti-vaxxer. That being said, fully vaccinated does not mean fully protected (against all the variant strains). Even fully vaccinated patients may need Ivermectin if they get sick with a variant.

Q. Are you saying the world and our country could open up immediately if everyone had access and accurate and open information on Ivermectin?

Frequently Asked Questions

A. Yes. Absolutely.

Q. Are you saying that the COVID-19 crisis in India would end if there were immediate and widespread prevention and treatment with Ivermectin?

A. Yes. Absolutely. Within weeks of Ivermectin's widespread use, we would expect to see that. Just look at what Czech Republic cases did after they adopted it. They plummeted. Now, look at Mexico. Within weeks of implementing the Ivermectin, their cases dissipated.

Ivermectin Added in Czechoslovakia: COVID Cases Drop

Czeck Republic
COVID-19 Deaths

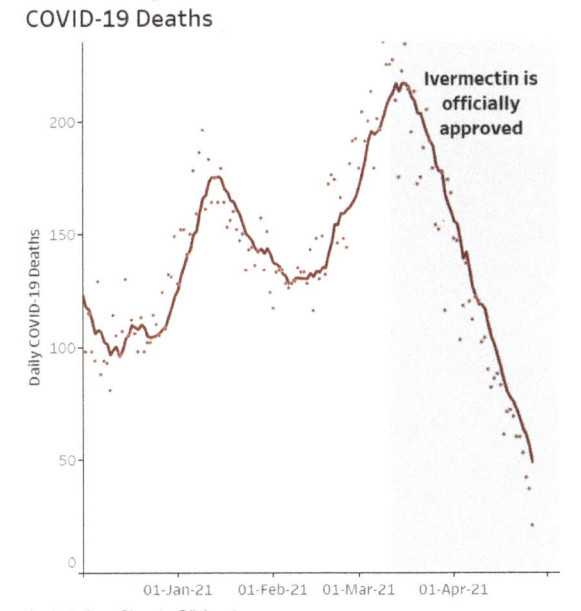

Analyst: Juan Chamie @jjchamie
Source: Ministery of Health Czech Republic

Ivermectin Added & Cases Evaporate

Ivermectin Added in Mexico: Cases Fall

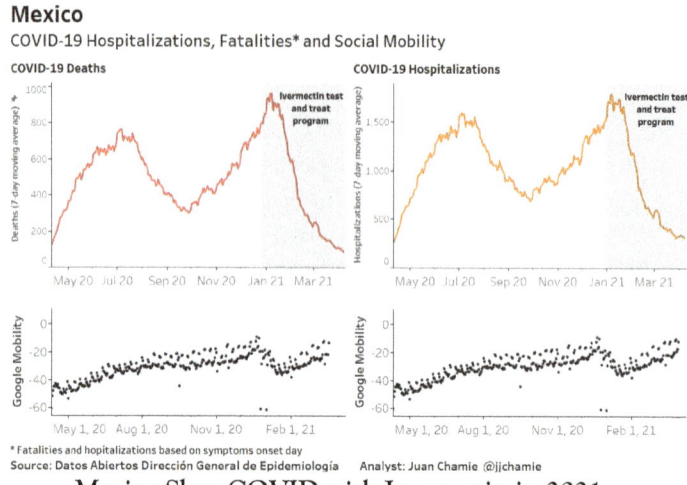

Mexico Slays COVID with Ivermectin in 2021

After Ivermectin Started in Peru, Cases Decline

Now do the opposite. Look at the country of Peru back in the fall of 2020.

When health minister Mazzetti initiated Ivermectin's widespread use in August, the COVID deaths dropped like a stone. Within weeks of this new Ivermectin policy, Peru's pandemic was tamed – without vaccines.

Frequently Asked Questions

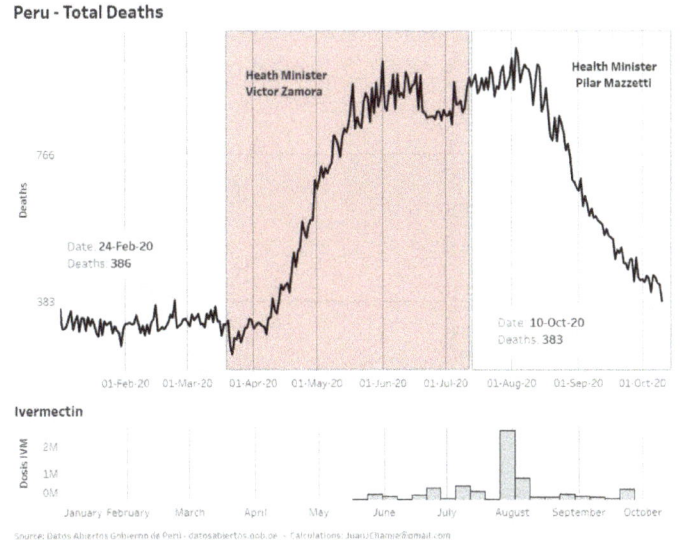

After Ivermectin Started & Cases Decline

Ivermectin Opponent Elected & Peru Cases Again Surge

Look at how the Peru cases surged after they elected a President who stopped Ivermectin.

President Francisco Sagasti came to power in Peru in November of 2020, and he was strongly backed by the UK, the USA, and the European Union. These allies conditioned their support of the new president upon promoting vaccines. Naturally, he opposed Ivermectin, and in January of 2021, he outlawed its use.

COVID-19 cases once again rapidly returned, and they now are once again surging. Add Ivermectin, and watch cases fall like clockwork. Subtract it and they skyrocket. You do the math.

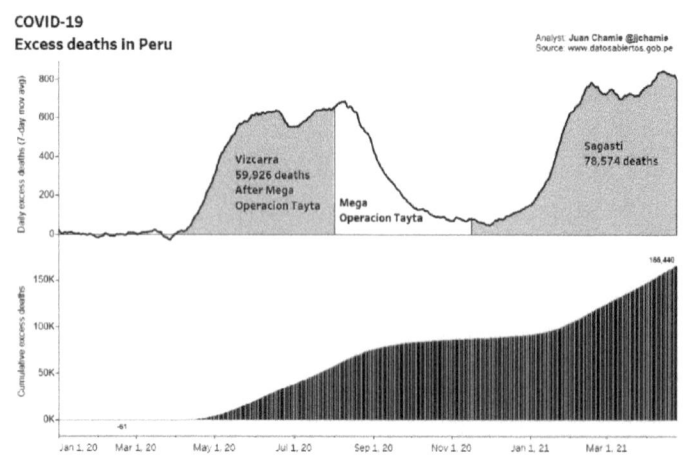

Ivermectin for the World

COVID-19
Excess deaths in Peru

Analyst: Juan Chamie @jjchamie
Source: www.datosabiertos.gob.pe

Vizcarra
59,926 deaths
After Mega
Operacion Tayta

Mega
Operacion Tayta

Sagasti
78,574 deaths

Sagasti Outlaws Ivermectin & Pandemic Roars Back

Always use common sense when you evaluate the data. Do not be a lamb led down the garden path and believe everything you hear or read. Think critically. And remember that powerful economic interests like Big Tobacco can lie to people for years, even decades if there is enough money involved.

They can always find scientists willing to twist the truth for enough money. There is talk about mandatory vaccinations now yearly for the entire US population. There is more talk about a third booster shot.

For corporations in the business of peddling prescription drugs, there is no greater opportunity than an unlimited supply of customers – matching the earth's population - required to purchase your product each and every year for as they long as they live. To what lengths might such a business go to protect such an opportunity?

Frequently Asked Questions

India's Cases Go Viral

Daily cases and deaths in Uttar Pradesh
Rolling seven-day averages

Cases

Deaths

Source: Ministry of Health and Family Welfare, data to 19 Apr — BBC

Indian Cases Go Viral

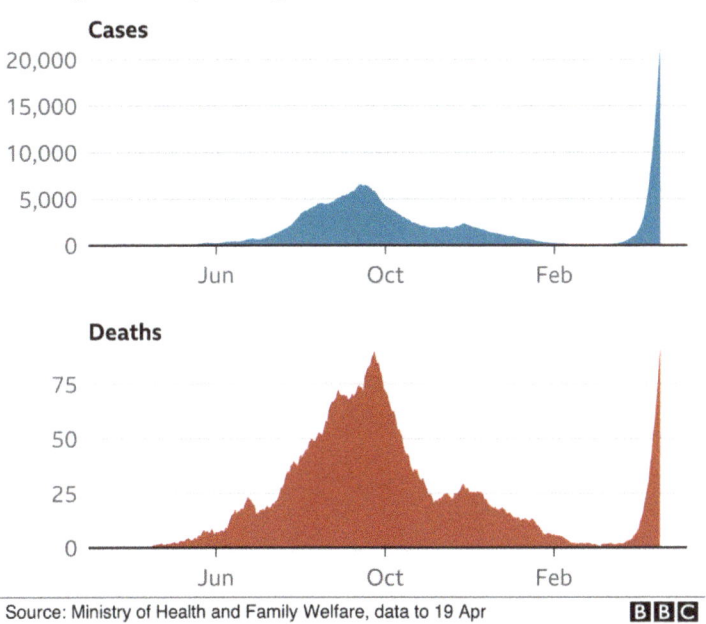

Imagine what would occur if Ivermectin were immediately added. You and your church can make this happen. Speak up. Speak out. Do something. We owe it to those innocent people who are dying in India. Remember the words of the great John Lewis:

By Congressman John Lewis
1940-2020

Co-Organizer of the 1963 March on Washington
Co-Leader of the 1965 March on Selma
Presidential Medal of Freedom Award
Robert F. Kennedy Book Award
John F. Kennedy Profile in Courage Award

"When you see something that isn't right – isn't fair, that isn't just – you have a moral obligation to say something, to do something."

AFTERWORD

Just days after completing this book, Dr. Tess Lawrie gave a stirring address at the first International Ivermectin for COVID Conference. With unwavering courage, she called out the corrupt organizations, including the WHO, Big Pharma, Big Regulators, and demanded an overhaul of the way clinical trials are conducted.

Dr. Lawrie publicly announced to the academic world that "millions of lives have been lost" due to corporate greed in suppressing the use of repurposed drugs in this pandemic. Furthermore, she observed that these colossal interests were holding medical doctors hostage.

There was no longer any doubt about corruption, tainted studies, and the link between Big Pharma, vaccinations, repurposed drug marginalization, and pandemic deaths. This could no longer be passed off as a conspiracy theory.

Dr. Tess Lawrie, Dr. Pierre Kory, and the BIRD research panel were now naming names.

It was no longer just a couple of doctors from the Imperial Valley of California. It was not merely a writer who published his articles as letters to the editor in *The Desert Review*. It was no longer just an eccentric French virologist or an Orthodox Jewish doctor from New York. Now it was a WHO consultant calling the WHO out. It was now mainstream knowledge.

Now the world would find out. And India might get Ivermectin. This leaves no doubt for the readers of this book on the correct course of action. What we could not do for America, we can now do for India.

You, the readers, the great conscience of America and the world, have the power and right to demand Ivermectin not only for India but also for your grandfather, grandmother, parents, yourself, and children.

So spread the word and let us all right this crime against humanity before it can claim one more life.

Make sure everyone knows about Ivermectin.

Justus R. Hope, MD

Redding, California

May 1, 2021

Dr. Tess Lawrie:
The Conscience of Medicine

Originally published May 1, 2021

Dr. Tess Lawrie Lights the Path

History is highlighted by turning points, moments of brilliance in the journey of humanity, episodes that changed civilization. These junctures often took place at times of great tragedy, during wars, famines, plagues, and revolution. Because at precisely those times, when the worst of human depravity became evident, we also witnessed the emergence of some of our greatest humanitarians, those who withstood opposition with grace and wisdom.

As steel is forged in a blast furnace, the best in humanity can only arise out of its cruelest chapters.

Oskar Schindler, a Nazi, gave away all his wealth to safeguard vulnerable Jewish people out of harm's way, away from the gas chambers. Oskar devoted his life at significant personal risk to saving others less fortunate; this is perhaps the fundamental principle of humanity.

Mohandas Gandhi raised a family as a successful lawyer in South Africa, yet chose to return to India to stop genocide. He traded a life of comfort for one of fasting, nonviolent protests, and personal risk. An assassin's bullet took his life in 1948, but not before he had spent 78 years on the planet and changed it forever. He is revered by many as the Father of India. His nonviolent protests to further social change inspired others to do the same, like Martin Luther King Jr, Robert Kennedy, and Nelson Mandela.

Nelson Mandela paid his price of tribulation with 27 years in a prison cell, one without a bed or plumbing. He spent his days breaking rocks and his free time writing. His manuscripts were scrutinized, restricted, censored, or destroyed. Nonetheless, he smuggled out a 500-page autobiography in 1976 and led a protest movement for prison rights.

This expanded into the anti-apartheid movement in South Africa. Out of Mandela's great suffering arose the principle of racial equality for South Africa, where he would ultimately be elected its first president. He remains affectionately known today as Madiba and is widely regarded as the Father of the Nation. He won the Nobel Peace Prize in 1993 for his nonviolent protests that proved victorious in ending the apartheid regime.

Afterword: Dr. Tess Lawrie

Dr. Tess Lawrie is a world-class researcher and consultant to The World Health Organization. Her biggest clients happen to be those who are involved in the suppression of repurposed drugs. She has decided to speak out in protest against the current medical establishment at considerable personal risk.

She co-founded the BIRD panel, an international group of experts dedicated to the transparent and accurate scientific research of Ivermectin. On April 24, 2021, she convened the International Ivermectin for COVID Conference, the first such symposium in the world held to focus on Ivermectin to prevent and treat COVID-19.

During the conference, she delivered a monumental closing address, one that will be recorded in the annals of medical history.

"They who design the trials and control the data also control the outcome. So this system of industry-led trials needs to be put to an end. Data from ongoing and future trials of novel COVID treatments must be independently controlled and analyzed. Anything less than total transparency cannot be trusted."

Dr. Lawrie called for reform of the method used to analyze scientific evidence.

She reported, "The story of Ivermectin has highlighted that we are at a remarkable juncture in medical history. The tools that we use to heal and our connection with our patients are being systematically undermined by relentless disinformation stemming from corporate greed. The story of Ivermectin shows that we as a public have misplaced our trust in the authorities and have underestimated the extent to which money and power corrupts.

Had Ivermectin being employed in 2020 when medical colleagues around the world first alerted the authorities to its efficacy, millions of lives could have been saved, and the pandemic with all its associated suffering and loss brought to a rapid and timely end."

Dr. Lawrie called out the corruption of modern medicine by Big Pharma and other interests.

She went on, "Since then, hundreds of millions of people have been involved in the largest medical experiment in human history. Mass vaccination was an unproven novel therapy. Hundreds of billions will be made by Big Pharma and paid for by the public. With politicians and other nonmedical individuals dictating to us what we are allowed to prescribe to the ill, we as doctors, have been put in a position such that our ability to uphold the Hippocratic oath is under attack.

At this fateful juncture, we must therefore choose, will we continue to be held ransom by corrupt organizations, health authorities, Big Pharma, and billionaire sociopaths, or will we do our moral and professional duty to do no harm and always do the best for those in our care? The latter includes urgently reaching out to colleagues around the world to discuss which of our tried and tested safe older medicines can be used against COVID."

Finally, Dr. Lawrie suggested that physicians form a new World Health Organization that represents the

Afterword: Dr. Tess Lawrie

interests of the people, not corporations and billionaires, a people-centered organization.

"Never before has our role as doctors been so important because never before have we become complicit in causing so much harm."

Dr. Albert Schweitzer would be proud. A Nobel laureate from 1952, Dr. Schweitzer won the Nobel Prize not for his work as a renowned medical missionary physician, but "for his altruism, reverence for life, and tireless humanitarian work which has helped make the idea of brotherhood between men and nations a living one."

While Mandela and King fought for equality in human rights, Dr. Schweitzer is most remembered for his principle of the ethic of "reverence for life."

Schweitzer wrote, "Ethics is nothing other than reverence for life. Reverence for life affords me my fundamental principle of morality, namely, that good consists of maintaining, assisting and enhancing life, and to destroy, harm or hinder life is evil."

Dr. Tess Lawrie knows that scientifically, Ivermectin saves lives. But moreover, she knows beyond any doubt that corruption has prevented Ivermectin from saving millions, caused untold suffering and horror, and a human economic toll of unimaginable proportions.

Out of this Pandemic have risen the true healers, those physicians who will be forever revered for risking their careers to save lives. When they could have remained silent and allowed the pandemic to take its course without rocking the boat, they chose to act.

Dr. George Fareed, Dr. Harvey Risch, and Dr. Peter McCullough traveled to the US Capitol and addressed the US Senate on November 19, 2020, and pleaded for the FDA and NIH to institute early outpatient treatment. They warned of the surge in deaths that would come. No answer. However, now during the current deadly second surge in India, on April 22, the Indian Council of Medical Research has just adopted Ivermectin and Budesonide for early outpatient therapy.

So why couldn't the US have done the same and heed the advice of Fareed and others, and with the stroke of a pen in November accord Ivermectin Emergency Use Authorization? Fully 300,000 lives could have been saved.

These physicians are the pandemic humanitarians; to Dr. George Fareed, who stood up to Dr. Anthony Fauci; to Dr. Brian Tyson, who borrowed 250,000 dollars in a personal loan to save the Imperial Valley; and to Dr. Harvey Risch, who risked his professorship at Yale to speak out.

To Dr. Peter McCullough of Texas, who authored the first study on early outpatient treatment. To Dr. Pierre Kory, who put his career on the line. To Dr. Tess Lawrie, physician, humanitarian, and reformer, who is leading the path to victory over the pandemic, a beacon of hope for human rights and the conscience of medicine.

Epilogue: India's Natural Experiment

Today is June 5, 2021, as I bring an optimistic update to all readers. Since this book's publication on May 1, exactly five weeks ago, we have witnessed nothing less than a miracle as India's COVID-19 crisis has evaporated – in those areas that adopted Ivermectin.

I must thank all the readers for their prayers and monumental efforts in sharing the message of this book far and wide. We succeeded!

The purpose of this has been to get the word out that "Ivermectin works" in the humble words of Dr. Hector Carvallo. The purpose of this book began to save India in it's humanitarian crisis. Now the message has broadened, and it is to do for the world what we did for India. For those readers who are seeing this information for the first time, allow me to reveal what just occurred with India.

At the end of April, India's cases have risen exponentially with no sign of slowing, and deaths were nearly 4,000 per day. New cases were nearly 400,000 per day. There was a shortage of oxygen and hospital space, and patients expired while waiting in front of hospitals. Less than a few percent of India had been vaccinated, and the country was staring a potential one million casualties in the face. But then something extraordinary happened. Something wonderful. Something incredible.

This is what the graph in Uttar Pradesh revealed six weeks ago. Then, there was no hope in sight.

Ivermectin for the World

This is what the graph in Uttar Pradesh revealed six weeks ago. Then, there was no hope in sight.

Daily cases and deaths in Uttar Pradesh
Rolling seven-day averages

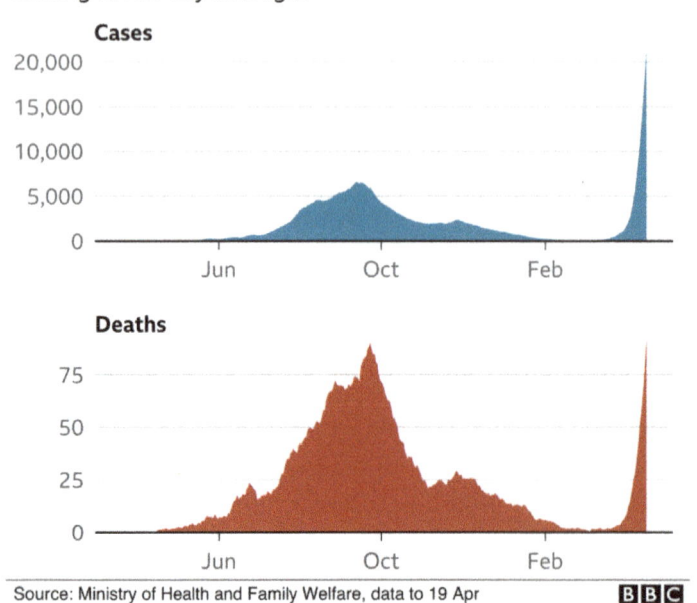

Source: Ministry of Health and Family Welfare, data to 19 Apr — BBC

BEFORE IVERMECTIN

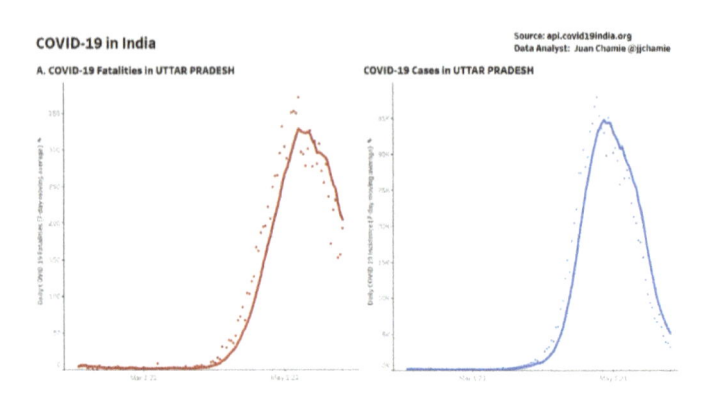

COVID-19 in India
A. COVID-19 Fatalities in UTTAR PRADESH
COVID-19 Cases in UTTAR PRADESH
Source: api.covid19india.org
Data Analyst: Juan Chamie @jjchamie

AFTER IVERMECTIN–Courtesy of Juan Chamie

Epilogue: India's Natural Experiment

Uttar Pradesh, a state that had dabbled previously, began mass distribution of Ivermectin following the AIIMS/ICMR guideline addition on April 20, 2021. Following this, cases dropped like a stone. Uttar Pradesh went from a peak of 37,944 on April 24th to 1,027 on June 5th – a drop of 97%.

However, my focus has been on Delhi, where cases peaked at 28,395 on April 20, the day of the AIIMS and ICMR announcement, adding Ivermectin. Cases today are 414 – an astounding drop of 99%.

Juan Chamie, the Cambridge data analyst who created many of these graphs, quoted a doctor who practices in Delhi.

Dr. Rajesh Chawla is a Pulmonologist practicing at the Apollo Hospital in New Delhi located in Delhi, India. On June 1st he reported, "In the last five days, I have seen only one COVID-19 case, and the patient was not from Delhi." Juan Chamie reports that the COVID-19 positivity rate is less than 1%, meaning very few have enough virus to spread. That rate was 20% one month ago, before the Ivermectin.

Ivermectin lowers the viral load, and thus we would expect widespread use of Ivermectin to stop spread as we have seen in Delhi. Juan Chamie's graph capture's this. So I refer to it as "The Ivermectin Effect," which is noticeable in all countries that adopt it.

COVID-19 in India

A. COVID-19 Fatalities in DELHI

COVID-19 Cases in DELHI

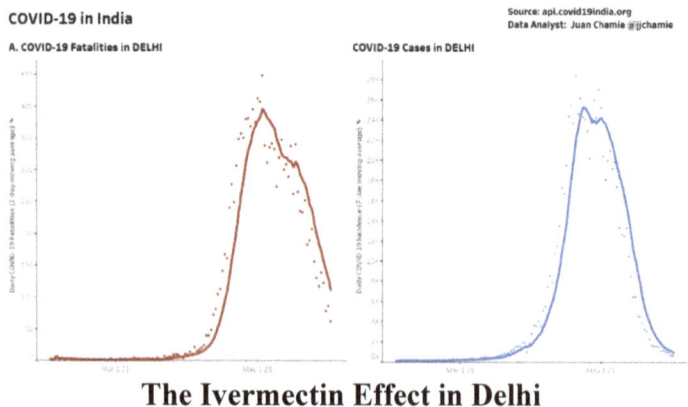

Source: api.covid19india.org
Data Analyst: Juan Chamie @jjchamie

**The Ivermectin Effect in Delhi
– Courtesy of Juan Chamie**

Other Indian states were to publicly announce their adoption of Ivermectin policies later in May, and the tiny state of Goa led these announcements on May 10, 2021. "So goes Goa, so goes the world" should be our motto. Three other Indian states quickly followed; Uttarakhand, Karnataka, and Tamil Nadu. All planned to adopt Ivermectin.

However, it was not to be for Tamil Nadu.

They elected a new leader, MK Stalin, and he listened to the WHO Chief Scientist, Dr. Soumya Swaminathan, who infamously tweeted a warning against its use on May 10, 2021. Dr. Swaminathan, a Pediatric Pulmonologist and expert in Tuberculosis, ironically was born in Madras which is modernly known as Tamil Nadu. She was born in the city of Chennai, the very same city where MK Stalin had served as Mayor.

Stalin was born in Chennai on March 1, 1953, while Swaminathan was born there on May 2, 1959. She has

Epilogue: India's Natural Experiment

served as the Chief Scientist for the WHO since 2019. She advised AGAINST the use of Ivermectin outside a clinical trial.

Tamil Nadu, therefore, outlawed Ivermectin and replaced it with Remdesivir shortly after they heard the WHO's advice. What followed is a classic natural experiment where a country or state adopts a drug, while another region outlaws it. Meaningful data may be obtained in this manner.

The results unfolded quickly. Cases in Tamil Nadu quickly tripled, and deaths rose ten-fold. Tamil Nadu's cases quickly exceeded all other states in India, and it became evident to all the world they had made the wrong choice. Tamil Nadu's cases peaked at 36,184 on May 21, after rising from 10,986 on April 20, 2021.

As the natural experiment played out, one could observe in real time during May as the cases and deaths dropped in those Indian states that chose Ivermectin. Cases in Uttarakhand, Goa, and Karnataka were examined closely, as this data would have broad applicability for the rest of the world.

Goa, one of the first states to adopt, announced it's Ivermectin plan on May 10, 2021. Goa cases peaked at 4,195 on May 7, and quickly fell. Today new cases are 567 – a drop of 86%.

https://www.hindustantimes.com/india-news/goa-wants-all-adults-to-take-ivermectin-here-s-why-fda-warned-against-its-use-101620711053627.html

Uttarakhand announced on May 12, their intention to use Ivermectin. Cases peaked at 9,642 on May 7, and today are down to 619 – a drop of 94%.

https://www.tribuneindia.com/news/nation/covid-19-ivermectin-tablets-to-be-distributed-among-uttarakhand-residents-says-state-govt-251832

Finally, our last state to examine in the natural experiment is Karnataka. Cases peaked on May 5 at 50,112 and are down to 13,800 today – a drop of 72%. Juan Chamie summarized the drop in India with the following graphic:

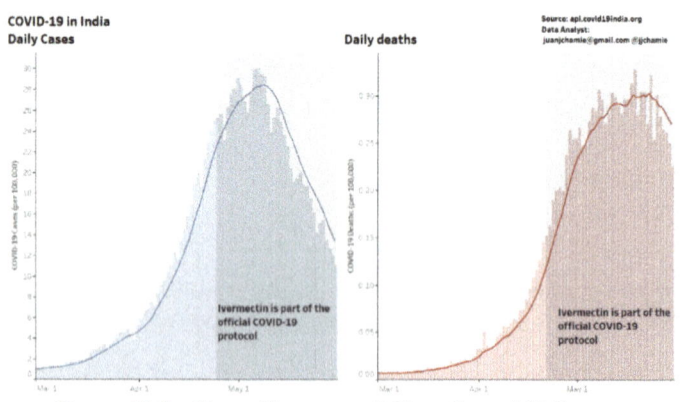

Overall Indian Cases and Death – All States – Courtesy of Juan Chamie

Naturally, Big Media and Big regulators tried to downplay all of this. They tried to explain it away by arguing the lockdowns worked, or the virus spread from the cities to the rural areas, or that the cases would have just fallen by themselves. But, unfortunately for them, none of these could explain

Epilogue: India's Natural Experiment

the vast divergences between the regions that chose Ivermectin and those that did not.

There was no way to explain away the profound effect of Ivermectin on the virus. It became obvious. It was self-evident from these graphs.

My articles in the Desert Review made it past the censors, and the message of India did not escape the world. The story of the Ivermectin Effect would become evident by this natural experiment, and no more "studies" offered by Big Pharma are necessary.

The jury is in, and Ivermectin works. And it works far better than the vaccines—a 99% drop in Delhi and a 98% drop in Uttar Pradesh.

You do not see that with the vaccines, not this quickly and not without adverse effects. Ivermectin is safe. We must now use it globally to bring an end to the Pandemic. And it works immediately. Hallelujah!

https://www.youtube.com/watch?v=UAx6oRcZK6Q

IVERMECTIN CRUSHES COVID IN DELHI

Originally published in the Desert Review on May 18, 2021

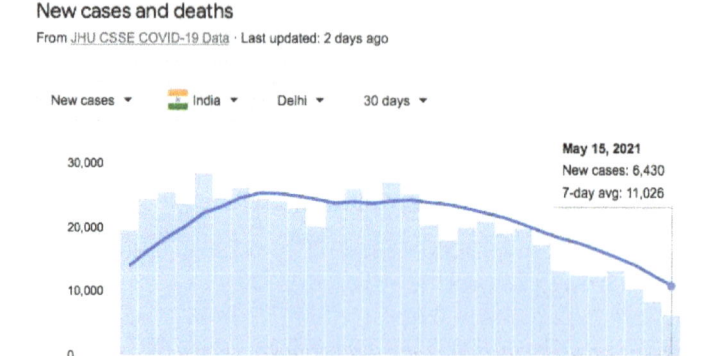

New cases and deaths
From JHU CSSE COVID-19 Data · Last updated: 2 days ago

[Chart showing New cases and 7-day average for India/Delhi over 30 days, with May 15, 2021: New cases: 6,430, 7-day avg: 11,026]

Delhi Cases Drop After Ivermectin Added

Just three weeks after adding Ivermectin, Delhi now leads India out of the deadly second surge of the COVID-19 pandemic. Cases plummeted nearly 80% between April 20 and May 15, dropping from 28,395 to just 6,430. Deaths are also down 25% from their peak.

On May 10, the Indian State of Goa adopted an even more ambitious policy of preemptive Ivermectin for all adults in the state. The Chief Minister of Goa is Dr. Pramod Sawant, a progressive 49-year-old physician persuaded by science. In particular, he read Dr. Pierre Kory's Dr. Tess Lawrie's and Dr. Andrew Hill's robust meta-analyses. As a direct result, Goa

Epilogue: India's Natural Experiment

has seen a 40% drop in cases from 3,124 the day after the announcement to 1,314 five days later.

Meanwhile, three other Indian states have followed Goa's lead in adding Ivermectin: Uttarkhand, Karnataka, and Uttar Pradesh. And, as expected, they have seen a drop in daily new cases as well, with Uttar Pradesh down nearly 75% - from a peak of 37,944 two days after the April 22 AIIMS guidance - to just 10,505 on May 16.

The All India Institute of Medical Sciences (AIIMS) announced new guidelines for COVID-19 that for the first time included Ivermectin use on April 22, 2021. The AIIMS protocol also listed hydroxychloroquine and Budesonide Inhaler. Both are drugs that Dr. George Fareed, former Harvard and NIH virologist, has been employing in California's Imperial Valley for more than one year with great success. Dr. Fareed's optimal cocktail includes Ivermectin, Fluvoxamine, Budesonide, and HCQ, along with nutraceuticals, including Zinc and Vitamin D3.

https://www.thedesertreview.com/health/local-frontline-doctors-modify-covid-treatment-based-on-results/article_9cdded9e-962f-11eb-a59a-f3e1151e98c3.html

The tragic story in all this is that the Indian state of Tamil Nadu installed a new leader on May 7, 2021. He suddenly reversed their state's decision to adopt Ivermectin. Readers of my book all know about Peruvian President Sagasti's fateful decision to outlaw Ivermectin. Before taking power, the COVID deaths had dropped 14 fold to almost nothing with

Ivermectin use. However, after Sagasti was elected, Ivermectin was stopped, and deaths roared back and rose 13 fold.

Peru paid the price in skyrocketing cases and 78,000 preventable deaths. Tamil Nadu's Chief Minister, MK Stalin, also chose to forgo Ivermectin. Instead, he ordered tens of thousands of doses of Remdesivir, a drug that sells for 3,000 dollars per dose. So now Tamil Nadu's cases are rocketing as well.

In contrast to Goa's young physician Chief Minister who had read the latest science on Ivermectin's dramatic effect on reducing COVID death, MK Stalin is a 68-year-old non-physician socialist and atheist who is towing the party line by forbidding Ivermectin.

Stalin now requests allocations for some 20,000 daily doses of Remdesivir for Tamil Nadu's citizens despite the scientific data that shows no reduction in COVID death with this drug. Remdesivir is an anti-viral agent given late in the disease, only after hospitalization when the Cytokine storm has set in and when anti-virals have lost their effectiveness.

At that late stage, steroids, anticoagulants, and oxygen are crucially important. Also, Ivermectin has shown a remarkable ability to reduce inflammation at that stage, with some patients being liberated from the ventilator with just a single dose.
Tamil Nadu's cases have continued to rise from April 20 to May 15. During that period, Delhi's cases eased 78% while Tamil Nadu's cases tripled.

Epilogue: India's Natural Experiment

Twenty thousand doses of Remdesivir cost 60 million dollars, while 20,000 doses of Ivermectin go for a few hundred. Where is a developing country getting the 60 million dollars a day to purchase the Remdesivir? Why is their leader throwing away a cheap drug, Ivermectin, that has saved lives in other countries?

Why would Stalin choose money over lives?

As a humanitarian and a board-certified practicing physician, I know we can influence other Indian states to adopt Ivermectin. With the help of groups like C19, the FLCCC, and the EBMC led by scientists of the caliber of Dr. Peter McCullough, Dr. George Fareed, Dr. Pierre Kory, and Dr. Tess Lawrie, let us all join together to get the word out. Ivermectin must be instituted globally to end not just the carnage in India but for the rest of the world.

This is life-saving information that everyone deserves to know - about how this Nobel Prize-winning drug, Ivermectin, can immediately bring an end to the pandemic. Tamil Nadu's citizens have a right to know the truth. It is everyone's human right to access it, and it is a drug for all of humanity. So help us fight the corruption and censorship. Please share the book, *Ivermectin for the World.*

TAMIL NADU LEADS INDIA IN NEW INFECTIONS; DENIES CITIZENS IVERMECTIN

Originally published in the Desert Review on May 21, 2021

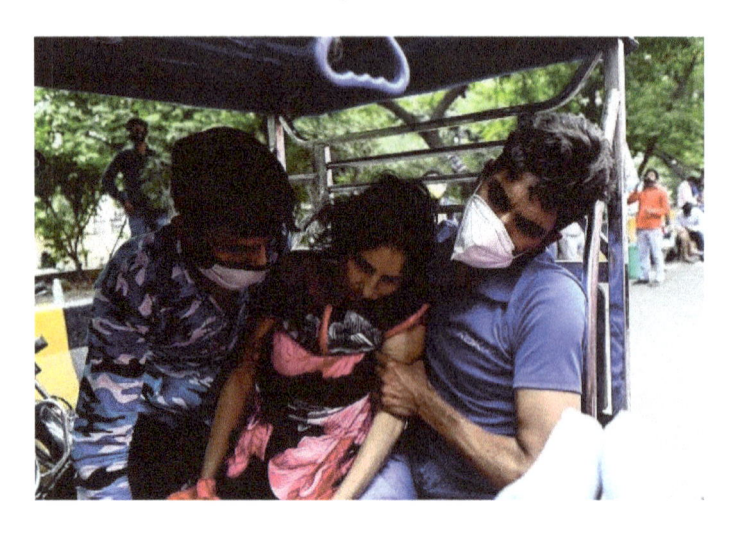

Tamil Nadu COVID Cases Rise to Record High - Getty Images

Tamil Nadu had the infamous distinction of leading India in new COVID-19 infections as of May 18, 2021,

"With 33,059 cases reported in the last 24 hours, Tamil Nadu is leading the state list," reported an article published in the Business Standard. May 19 was to be worse with 34,875 new infections, again

Epilogue: India's Natural Experiment

with the dubious distinction of being number one in India.

The Indian Express reported yet a further daily record increase to 35,579 new TN infections as of May 20. Tamil Nadu has outlawed Ivermectin use for COVID, which may explain their horrific rise in new COVID infections.

Meanwhile, cases in Delhi continue to fall as they douse their COVID flame with Ivermectin. As of May 19, 2021, Delhi's infections had plunged 87% from 28,395 on April 20 - when they began using Ivermectin - to just 3,846.

They began using Ivermectin when AIIMS announced adding Ivermectin to COVID-19 outpatient treatment, something my group, C19, has been calling for in the US since Dr. George Fareed, Dr. Peter McCullough, and Dr. Harvey Risch testified on November 19, 2020, to the US Senate. The trio advocated early outpatient treatment of the type Dr. Fareed and his associate Dr. Brian Tyson have used to save almost 6000 patients in California's Imperial Valley.

https://www.thedesertreview.com/health/local-frontline-doctors-modify-covid-treatment-based-on-results/article_9cdded9e-962f-11eb-a59a-f3e1151e98c3.html

This fell on deaf ears. Dr. Pierre Kory reiterated this plea on December 8, 2020. The NIH upgraded their guidance from "against Ivermectin" to "neutral," meaning neither for or against. The FDA remained firmly "against."

Had the NIH or FDA provided EUA or Emergency Use Authorization, fully 300,000 US lives would have been saved as a conservative estimate.

However, what we could not do for America, we proposed doing for India in our newest plea contained in the book, *Ivermectin for the World*. Released on May 1, 2021, the book called for every reader to pray, protest or pressure their governments and representatives to urge India to adopt Ivermectin -for mass prevention, outpatient, and inpatient treatment to ease their COVID crisis - on humanitarian grounds.

The readers were influenced and have responded with massive assistance. I thank them.

Acknowledging that the ICMR and AIIMS had already added Ivermectin to their outpatient treatment protocol on April 20, 2021 with noticeable improvements in Uttar Pradesh and Delhi, a joint statement was issued by the FLCCC and the Evidence Based Medicine Consultancy on May 3 urging the immediate adoption of Ivermectin for prevention and treatment of COVID-19 by India and the world to put an end to the pandemic.

India's officials heard this message and acted further.

The states of Goa, Uttarakhand, Karnataka, and Tamil Nadu agreed to adopt Ivermectin. Goa led the way on May 10 with the announcement that every man and woman over 18 would receive 12 mg of Ivermectin daily for five days irrespective of COVID status. The world was finally moving in the right direction. Thank God!

Thank God, until an atheist and new Chief Minister, MK Stalin, took power on May 7, 2021, in Tamil Nadu and proclaimed that Remdesivir would replace Ivermectin as their drug of choice. Now Tamil Nadu's cases are diverging from the states that chose Ivermectin.

Goa's cases have dropped 62% in just nine days since announcing the Ivermectin policy - from 3124 down to 1204. The other Indian Ivermectin states have also enjoyed a substantial decrease in new infections. By contrast, Tamil's citizens face an ascending escalator of cases bringing untold misery and mortality to this southern Indian community, which begs the question - When will Tamil Nadu hear the message that Ivermectin saves lives? When will the rest of humanity take heed?

Is Ivermectin the New Penicillin?

Originally published in the Desert Review on May 25, 2021

Uttarakhand; As Far Away from Delhi as it Gets

As those Indian States using Ivermectin continue to diverge in cases and deaths from those states that forbid it, the natural experiment illustrates the power of Ivermectin decisively.

Cases in Delhi, where Ivermectin was begun on April 20, dropped from 28,395 to just

2,260 on May 22. This represents an astounding 92% drop. Likewise, cases in Uttar Pradesh have dropped from 37,944 on April 24 to 5,964 on May 22 - a decline of 84%.

Delhi and Uttar Pradesh followed the All India Institute of Medical Sciences (AIIMS) guidance published April 20, 2021, which called for dosing of .2 mg per kg of Ivermectin per body weight for three days. This amounts to 15 mg per day for a 150-pound person or 18 mg per day for a 200-pound individual.

The other three Indian states that adopted it are all down as well. Goa is down from 4,195 to 1,647, Uttarakhand is down from 9,624 to 2,903, and Karnataka is down from 50,112 to 31,183. Goa adopted a pre-emptive policy of mass Ivermectin prevention for the entire adult population over age 18 at a dose of 12 mg daily for five days.

Meanwhile, Tamil Nadu announced on May 14 they were outlawing Ivermectin in favor of the politically correct Remdesivir. As a result, Tamil Nadu's cases are up in the same time frame from April 20 to May 22 - 10,986 to 35,873 - more than a tripling.

Although Big Pharma and Big Media have scrambled to try, they cannot explain away this natural experiment. As I predicted May 12, they would first argue "the lockdowns worked." The problem with this is that Tamil Nadu has been on strict lockdown for weeks as their cases have done nothing but climb. So the lockdown did not work.
Their next argument was that "there has been a shift from the highly populated urban areas like Delhi and Mumbai" to the hinterlands, like Tamil Nadu. The big problem is that the adjacent state, Karnataka is just as rural, and its cases are dropping on Ivermectin.

Uttar Pradesh is near the Himalayas and out in the far non-urbanized north where cases are down 84% with Ivermectin. Uttarakhand is even more rural and located in the Himalayas next to Nepal. Its infections are down 70% with Ivermectin.

Their final argument lacked any proof. It was essentially an attempt to smear Ivermectin through association with another drug. It attempted to link Hydroxychloroquine (HCQ) with Ivermectin unfairly. While HCQ has become a punchline by the media, scientists like Dr. George Fareed know it is effective against COVID-19 – especially in the early stages.

Dr. Fareed and his associate, Dr. Brian Tyson, have treated some 6,000 patients with nearly 100% success using a combination of HCQ, Ivermectin, Fluvoxamine, and various nutraceuticals, including zinc Vitamin D.

https://www.thedesertreview.com/health/local-frontline-doctors-modify-covid-treatment-based-on-results/article_9cdded9e-962f-11eb-a59a-f3e1151e98c3.html

Unfortunately, none of this has made it through the censorship of the mainstream media, and the public has not heard about the 200 plus studies that reflect HCQ's effectiveness against COVID-19. The fact remains that HCQ has an undeserved negative connotation due to its connection with Trump, which is unfortunately used to tarnish other life-saving repurposed drugs, like Ivermectin. For example, in the recent Forbes article, journalist Ray uses the title, "Is Ivermectin the New Hydroxychloroquine?"

Epilogue: India's Natural Experiment

https://www.forbes.com/sites/siladityaray/2021/05/19/is-ivermectin-the-new-hydroxychloroquine-online-interest-in-unproven-covid-drug-surges-as-experts-urge-caution/

Ray does not make a single substantive argument against Ivermectin; instead, he attempts to defame, debase or degrade it by repeating baseless accusations. For example, Ray cited Merck's recommendation against Ivermectin as evidence of ineffectiveness, while Merck used no evidence to support their claim. In addition, he cited the FDA's recommendation against Ivermectin, yet the FDA admits they have not reviewed the data on which to base this conclusion: "The FDA has not reviewed data to support the use of Ivermectin in COVID-19 patients to treat or prevent COVID-19..."

As we all know, Merck was involved in the development of a competing drug and had 356 million reasons to throw its own cheap, unprofitable Ivermectin under the bus. Furthermore, the US government was likewise involved in a significant financial conflict of interest with Merck.

https://trialsitenews.com/is-the-ivermectin-situation-rigged-in-favor-of-industry-is-the-big-tobacco-analogy-appropriate/

The story of Ivermectin is more similar to that of Penicillin. Penicillin has saved almost 200 million lives. In addition, three men shared a Nobel Prize in 1945 for its discovery.

Ivermectin's discoverers won the 2015 Noble Prize in Medicine, and it has proven to be a life-saving drug in parasitic disease, especially in Africa. Over the past four decades, Ivermectin has saved millions from parasites like strongyloidiasis and onchocerciasis - river blindness.

It has already saved tens of thousands from COVID-19 in India in those few locations that use it. It crashed Mexico's, Slovakia's, and Zimbabwe's cases. I remain more convinced than ever that Ivermectin will bring an end to this Pandemic as the word gets out and more people share the book, *Ivermectin for the World*. A more fitting title to the Forbes piece might be, "Is Ivermectin the New Penicillin?"

IVERMECTIN OBLITERATES 97% OF DELHI CASES

*Originally published in the Desert Review
June 1, 2021*

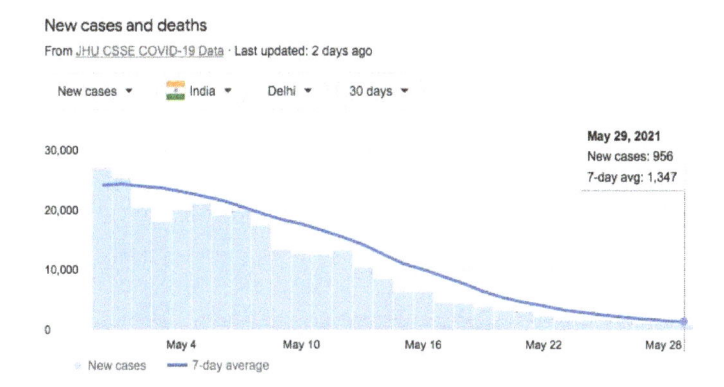

IVERMECTIN OBLITERATES DELHI COVID CASES

A 97% decline in Delhi cases with Ivermectin is decisive – period. It represents the last word in an epic struggle to save lives and preserve human rights. This graph symbolizes the victory of reason over corruption, good over evil, and right over wrong. It is as significant as David's victory over Goliath. It is an absolute vindication of Ivermectin and early outpatient treatment. It is a clear refutation of the WHO, FDA, NIH, and CDC's policies of "wait at home until you turn blue" before you get treatment.

Dr. Pierre Kory told the world on December 8, 2020, that Ivermectin "obliterates" this virus. Obliterate means to decimate, demolish, or annihilate. It means to eliminate or destroy all trace, indication, or significance.

This graph shows that Ivermectin, used in Delhi beginning April 20, obliterated their COVID crisis. No one should be able to talk you out of this - not a salesman, a drug company, a television celebrity doc, and certainly not the top doctor for the WHO or the NIH who is paid to do that.

Will you believe this 97% eradication graph, or will you believe the propaganda pitched by the Big Media, Big Pharma, the WHO, and the FDA, who share massive financial conflicts of interest – those who say there is insufficient evidence?

What evidence could be any clearer than a 97% reduction in five weeks? That number is better than the current vaccines and beyond the reach of most medicines.

The WHO cautioned India they were making a mistake by using Ivermectin. They told them it could be dangerous, that there was no evidence it worked. How many lies will you buy before you stand up for the truth?

The fatal mistake would have been to NOT use Ivermectin.

Mercifully they used it, and they saved Delhi. But tragically, Tamil Nadu did not, and their state was devastated. Their new cases rose from 10,986 to 36,184 – a tripling.

Epilogue: India's Natural Experiment

No one can hide that. Their refusal to use Ivermectin harmed them. Not only did Tamil Nadu's cases rise to the highest in India, but their deaths skyrocketed from 48 on April 20 to 474 on May 27 – a rise of ten-fold.

Meanwhile, Delhi's deaths IN THE SAME PERIOD fell from 277 to 117. So which advice would you have wanted your state to follow?

In America, Baylor's Dr. Peter McCullough, Yale's Dr. Harvey Risch, and Harvard's Dr. George Fareed first advised early outpatient treatment in testimony to the US Senate on November 19, 2021. Dr. McCullough and his colleagues were the first in the world to publish an early outpatient treatment protocol for COVID-19.

https://www.amjmed.com/article/S0002-9343(20)30673-2/fulltext

That protocol has since been revised by Dr. George Fareed and his dynamic associate, Dr. Brian Tyson. They have now saved 6,000 COVID patients in California's Imperial Valley.

https://www.thedesertreview.com/health/local-frontline-doctors-modify-covid-treatment-based-on-results/article_9cdded9e-962f-11eb-a59a-f3e1151e98c3.html

Less than one month later, Dr. Pierre Kory sounded the alarm for a second time on December 8, 2020, to the US Senate. He advised the use of Ivermectin, yet no one listened. No Ivermectin guidelines were instituted. On December 8, the US suffered 2,821 COVID deaths. With Ivermectin, cases could have been quickly crushed. Fatalities would have dropped in short order, as the example of Delhi shows us.

But instead, the United States followed the WHO and FDA's official advice and waited for the vaccines. They sat on their hands while people gasped. They watched and did nothing as millions turned blue and flooded the hospitals - no Ivermectin approval. So like Tamil Nadu, our US cases and deaths also skyrocketed.

By January 8, just four weeks later, US daily cases had risen from 219,000 to 300,000, and deaths were up from 2,821 to 3,895. Even more Americans were to die due to this failed health policy of ignoring Ivermectin and early outpatient treatment.

Delhi did it right. The United States and Tamil Nadu did it wrong. It cost half a million precious lives and horrific pain and suffering for the world. The pandemic was prolonged for no good reason.

Now we are in a different position. We as a people have absolute evidence of Ivermectin's efficacy. In Delhi, we heard not one single story of Ivermectin being toxic or causing any difficulty. On the contrary, it is safe, and it saved tens of thousands from COVID.

But more immediately, what can we do now? What will you do as a concerned citizen to get the word out? What can you do to save your fellow human beings from repeating these costly errors? Start with sharing the book, *Ivermectin for the World*, with your

Epilogue: India's Natural Experiment

church, your minister, and all your social contacts. Then, spread the word far and wide:

People can safely take Ivermectin to prevent and treat COVID-19.

The rest of the world must hear about Ivermectin as new areas experience similar surges. A new hybrid variant is brewing in Vietnam. Notify them! They need to know there is more than masks and social distancing. There is more than waiting for vaccines. Ivermectin is effective against ALL the variants. The vaccines ARE NOT.

But, unfortunately, the authorities will continue to censor this information; thus, the responsibility of getting the word out rests squarely upon the citizens of the planet, you and me.

https://www.amazon.com/Ivermectin-World-Justus-R-Hope-ebook/dp/B0943T564G

Lead a peaceful protest. Share this article with everyone you know, your social media, your email contacts, relatives, friends, and co-workers. You may think that none of this applies to you because you have already been vaccinated. That is unfortunately not true.

Listen to Dr. Peter McCullough on this subject. He is the Vice-Chair of Medicine at Baylor University Medical Center in Dallas, Texas. He is among the most published cardiologists in the world. He is arguably the most courageous physician to speak out.

https://vimeo.com/553518199

No one deserves COVID. No one deserves to die when we have effective treatment.

Do you continue to believe the pronouncements of those agencies that have failed you so many times before? Those agencies who have told the media to give you only filtered information, those agencies who have ignored the world's leading scientists.

Take a look at this graph. Delhi was in dire straits on April 20 with 28,395 new daily COVID-19 cases and rising.

We sounded the alarm. The All India Institute for Medical Science (AIIMS) and the Indian Council of Medical Research (ICMR) had the guts to listen. They listened to the 56 studies involving 18,447 patients showing up to a 91% reduction in death with Ivermectin. They listened to scientists like Dr. Pierre Kory and the FLCCC. They listened to world-class experts like Dr. Tess Lawrie of the BIRD group and Dr. Peter McCullough of the C19 group. They were smart.

The book *Ivermectin for the World* was released May 1, 2021, and called for the urgent adoption of Ivermectin by India on a humanitarian basis to save lives. "What we could not do for America, we can do for India!" was our mantra.

Epilogue: India's Natural Experiment

And we did! This is what happened to cases in the areas that chose Ivermectin:

Delhi :	↓ 97%	[28,395 to 956]
Uttar Pradesh:	↓ 95%	[37,944 to 2,014]
Goa:	↓ 85%	[4195 to 645]
Karnataka:	↓ 60%	[50,112 to 20,378]
Uttarakhand:	↓ 87%	[9,642 to 1,226]

Observe what happened to those areas that DID NOT choose Ivermectin:

Tamil Nadu	↑ 173%	[10,986 to 30,016]
Odisha	↑ 50%	[4,761 to 7,148]
Assam	↑ 240%	[1,651 to 5,613]
Arunachal Pradesh	↑ 656%	[61 to 461]
Tripura	↑ 828%	[92 to 854]

On May 3, the FLCCC and the BIRD groups issued a press release and called for the immediate global use of Ivermectin for COVID-19. On May 7, Dr. Paul Marik, the second most published Intensive Care Specialist in the world and founding member of the FLCCC, did the same. He added that we could no longer trust "larger health authorities to make an honest examination of the medical and scientific evidence."

https://eurekalert.org/pub_releases/2021-05/fccc-lpr050621.php

In India, the acid test was to compare the fates of those Indian areas that adopted the drug versus those that did not. This would be the ultimate natural experiment. Finally, the plain truth would be revealed to all the world. It was no longer the special interests, Big Pharma, Big Regulators, and Big Media, who had been censoring, swindling, and conniving. Now the fight would be fair because all the money in the world could not conceal the cases in Delhi. The world had a front-row seat to witness these results. And it bears repeating; the results are in.

Delhi's cases are down 97% from 28,395 on April 20 to just 956 on May 29.

So the question now is this: Are you going to believe the obvious contained in these graphs? Or are you going to believe those corrupt agencies that do not have your best interests at heart, those who have lied to you many times before?

I suggest you believe the scientists from non-profit groups like FLCCC and BIRD who have nothing to gain except saving your life. They are the most trustworthy. You can support Dr. Tess Lawrie's charitable work at:

https://www.gofundme.com/f/help-us-get-lifesaving-drug-approved-for-covid19

You can support Dr. Pierre Kory's charitable work on:

https://covid19criticalcare.com/

You can support Dr. George Fareed's charitable work and his COVID-19 project by contributing to www.holtvillebaptist.com in the name of the COVID-19 Fareed Project. Dr. George Fareed is a voice of wisdom.

Epilogue: India's Natural Experiment

https://youtu.be/czJuCCBIoX4

Dr. Fareed is a former NIH scientist and Harvard Professor. He holds patents on three cancer drugs. He was named the 2015 California Rural Physician of the Year, and he won the Plessner Memorial Award given by the California Medical Association for his ethics and clinical excellence. So, you can trust and believe Dr. Fareed.

https://youtu.be/7pKBfRHFJAg

The choice is clear. Ivermectin is the safe, repurposed Nobel Prize-Winning drug that effectively reduces death up to 91% from COVID-19. It does not produce blood clots, heart attacks, or strokes. It does not cause violent immune reactions. And it reduced the COVID-19 cases in Delhi, India, by an astonishing 97% in five weeks. It costs pennies.

Tell the poor citizens of Tamil Nadu who are still in the dark and remain forbidden from using it. Tell the rest of the world. Show your doctor the studies. They are updated daily on www.ivmmeta.com. If your doctor refuses, find another doctor.

Listen to scientists and physicians who are driven by their Hippocratic Oaths to do what is right, not the doctors who are paid vast sums of money by lucrative interests to tow the party line.

So the next time you hear a highly paid doctor advising you that Ivermectin does not work, or you read another article disputing this, please believe your eyes and this graph.

Use your common sense. Some truths are self-evident, and Ivermectin's pronounced effect against this virus is one of them. Another self-evident truth, straight from the Declaration of Independence, is the human right to life - which includes the right to select medical treatment - free from governmental interference.

We do not require scientists to interpret these fundamental truths. We do not need a philosopher to know that censorship of life-saving information is wrong. We do not require any more "studies" to understand that all the world needs Ivermectin - immediately.

"What we did for India, we must now do for the rest of the world!"

https://youtu.be/UAx6oRcZK6Q

Indian Bar Association Sues WHO Scientist Over Ivermectin

Originally published June 6, 2021

The World Health Organization

On May 25, 2021, the Indian Bar Association (IBA) sued WHO Chief Scientist Dr. Soumya Swaminathan, accusing her in a 71 point brief of causing the deaths of Indian citizens by misleading them about Ivermectin. Point 56 states,

"That your misleading tweet on May 10, 2021, against the use of Ivermectin had the effect of the State of Tamil Nadu withdrawing Ivermectin from the protocol on May 11, 2021, just a day after the Tamil Nadu government had indicated the same for the treatment of COVID-19 patients."

https://science.thewire.in/health/tn-revises-protocols-leaves-out-Ivermectin-for-covid-patients/

Advocate Dipali Ojha, lead attorney for the Indian Bar Association, threatened criminal prosecution against Dr. Swaminathan "for each death" caused by her acts of commission and omission. The brief accused Swaminathan of misconduct by using her position as a health authority to further the agenda of special interests to maintain an EUA for the lucrative vaccine industry.

https://indianbarassociation.in/press-releases/

Specific charges included the running of a disinformation campaign against Ivermectin and issuing statements in social and mainstream media to wrongfully influence the public against the use of Ivermectin despite the existence of large amounts of clinical data showing its profound effectiveness and both prevention and treatment of COVID-19.

In particular, the Indian Bar Brief referenced the peer-reviewed publications and evidence compiled by the ten-member FLCCC group and the 65-member BIRD panel headed by WHO consultant and meta-analysis expert Dr. Tess Lawrie.

The brief cited US Attorney Ralph C. Lorigo's hospital cases in New York where court orders were required for dying COVID patients to receive the Ivermectin. In multiple instances of such comatose patients, following the court-ordered Ivermectin, the patients recovered. In addition, the Indian Bar Association cited previous articles published in this forum, *The Desert Review*.

Epilogue: India's Natural Experiment

Advocate Ojha accused the WHO and Dr. Swaminathan in Points 60 and 61 as having misled and misguided the Indian people throughout the pandemic from mask wear to exonerating China as to the virus's origins.

"The world is gradually waking up to your absurd, arbitrary and fallacious approach in presenting concocted facts as "scientific approach." While the WHO flaunts itself like a "know it all," it is akin to the vain Emperor in new clothes while the entire world has realized by now, the Emperor has no clothes at all.

The brief accused the WHO of being complicit in a vast disinformation campaign. Point 61 states,

"The FLCCC and the BIRD have shown exemplary courage in building a formidable force to tackle the challenge of disinformation, resistance, and rebuke from pharma lobbies and powerful health interests like WHO, NIH, CDC, and regulators like the US FDA."

Dr. Swaminathan was called out for her malfeasance in discrediting Ivermectin to preserve the EUA for the vaccine and pharmaceutical industry. Point 52 reads, "It seems you have deliberately opted for deaths of people to achieve your ulterior goals, and this is a sufficient grounds for criminal prosecution against you."

The IBA posted an update on their website June 5, 2021, noting that Dr. Swaminathan had deleted her now-infamous tweet. They wrote, "However, deleting the tweet will not save Dr. Soumya Swaminathan and her associates from the criminal prosecution which is to be launched by the citizens with active support from the Indian Bar Association."

https://indianbarassociation.in/blogs-iba/

In this update, the Advocate Dipali Ojha clarified the nature of the planned action,

"The Indian Bar Association has warned action under section 302 etc. of the Indian Penal Code against Dr. Soumya Swaminathan& others, for murder of each person dying due to obstruction in treatment of COVID-19 patient effectively by Ivermectin. Punishment under section 302 of the Indian Penal Code is death penalty or life imprisonment."

He further wrote, "After receiving the said notice, Dr. Soumya Swaminathan went on the back foot and deleted her tweet. This has proved the hollowness of the WHO's recommendation against Ivermectin for COVID-19. The dishonesty of WHO and the act of Dr. Soumya Swaminathan in deleting her contentious tweet was witnessed by netizens across the world, as the news got a wide coverage on social media. By deleting the tweet, Dr. Soumya Swaminathan has proved her mala fide intentions."

The entire world witnessed the effectiveness of Ivermectin against India's deadly second surge as the locations that adopted it saw their outbreaks quickly extinguished in stark contrast to those states that did not.

Epilogue: India's Natural Experiment

Among the most prominent examples include the Ivermectin areas of Delhi, Uttar Pradesh, Uttarakhand, and Goa where cases dropped 98%, 97%, 94%, and 86%, respectively. By contrast, Tamil Nadu opted out of Ivermectin. As a result, their cases skyrocketed and rose to the highest in India. Tamil Nadu deaths increased ten-fold.

https://www.thedesertreview.com/news/national/ivermectin-obliterates-97-percent-of-delhi-cases/article_6a3be6b2-c31f-11eb-836d-2722d2325a08.html

Tamil Nadu publicly relied upon Dr. Swaminathan's advice in revoking their initial choice of Ivermectin the day after she recommended against it in her May 10 tweet on social media. As a direct result, Tamil Nadu experienced a surge in COVID death and sickness that continues to this day.

The Indian Bar Association dared to initiate a landmark court case against a Public Health Authority (PHA) to call out corruption and to save lives. As the courts in the United States proved to be the life-saving force to ensure a patient's right to receive Ivermectin, a court in India is now doing the same.

Criminal prosecution of public health officials will send a powerful signal that disinformation campaigns resulting in death carry consequences. Perhaps this pathway will ultimately break the disinformation and censorship stranglehold around repurposed drug use to save lives. Maybe we will witness other countries following India's example, both in medicine and in law.

POST-SCRIPT: CANCER & VIRUSES

In closing, allow me to share something that is never mentioned enough. Many may not know this, but what is important here is one thing: Repurposed Drug Cocktails work against viruses – And Repurposed Drug Cocktails work against Terminal Cancer.

And they work spectacularly well.

The other important thing to remember is this: Big Pharma controls Big Regulators and can manipulate the studies to show anything they wish.

And Big Pharma will always protect their Chemotherapy Industry. It is worth billions. You can expect them and their brethren, the FDA, CDC, and NIH to ALWAYS be opposed to safe, cheap, repurposed drug cocktails for cancer regardless of whether they work.

Patients are dying every day from terminal cancer; cancers of the pancreas, the brain, blood, lymph, and organs, and these cancers SHOULD ALWAYS have repurposed drug cocktails added. If they do not result in a cure, they will almost always give the person more months or years of life.

Just because your oncologist says "no" or laughs, please, please, ask your family doctor to consider adding them. Get Jane McClelland's book or my other book, but whatever you do, DO NOT settle for the standard of care. Because after devoting the better

Post-Script: Cancer & Viruses

part of two years to the study of repurposed drugs, I have become convinced they are effective.

I must take this opportunity to thank Dr. Harvey Risch, the first doctor to speak out about repurposed drugs for use against COVID-19. Dr. Risch is the Distinguished Professor of Epidemiology at the Yale School of Public Health, and he serves as the Associate Editor for the Journal of the National Cancer Institute. He is the man who answered my email in less than five minutes on a Saturday evening, and he is the original, courageous leader in this Pandemic.

He stood tall against all the forces of the NIH, the CDC, the FDA, and Dr. Fauci to save lives despite any risk to his career. Before Dr. Tess Lawrie and Dr. Peter McCullough took their bold stands, Dr. Risch led the fight and took the bullets. Had the United States followed his straightforward advice in June of 2020, we could have saved more than half a million lives. Dr. Risch remains the ultimate leader and the earliest voice for repurposed drugs in this Pandemic.

I must take this opportunity to thank Dr. George Fareed, who has become a mentor to me. Dr. Fareed pioneered the first AIDS clinic in Brawley, California. The community is so blessed to have him. Dr. Fareed prescribed repurposed drug cocktails to AIDS patients BEFORE the studies had come out, before AZT.

So George already knew it before the world figured out that multi-drug cocktails were essential in making AIDS a long-term survivable disease. George was correct that these common collections of daily pills could stop the AIDS virus. He was also stunningly accurate that a multi-drug cocktail could stop COVID-19 – starting with that controversial drug, HCQ.

It is not dangerous, and it is effective against COVID-19.

And Dr. Fareed and his associate, Dr. Tyson, showed the world this truth, another self-evident one, by saving 6,000 patients in the Imperial Valley with a cocktail comprised not of a single drug, but a collection:

https://www.thedesertreview.com/health/local-frontline-doctors-modify-covid-treatment-based-on-results/article_9cdded9e-962f-11eb-a59a-f3e1151e98c3.html

HCQ, Ivermectin, Zinc, Doxycycline, Azithromycin, Aspirin, monoclonal antibodies, and Vitamin D3.

Why?

Great question. Please read the answer carefully – because if you ever get cancer, you will want to remember this. Viruses like cancers are resilient, and they are capable of mutating and evading your Big Gun million-dollar drug. Give them enough exposure and time, and they will constantly evolve resistance. NEVER, EVER rely on one drug whether you are being treated for terminal cancer or COVID-19. Add at the very least a strategically chosen supplement.

Post-Script: Cancer & Viruses

They also help block resistance. Don't be fooled into thinking it must require a prescription.

Dr. Fareed ALWAYS uses a combination because reliance upon a single drug is asking for failure. When a patient gets the standard cancer treatment of surgery, radiation, and the latest and greatest chemotherapy, we ALWAYS leave the back door open for a resistant strain to emerge and return to harm us.

For COVID-19, it is no different. That is why Dr. Jackie Stone of Zimbabwe always treats her COVID patients with additional drugs besides Ivermectin. She adds Doxycycline or HCQ. Dr. Paul Marik developed the I-MASK+ protocol. It contains many other substances besides Ivermectin and includes Zinc, D3, Melatonin, C, Zinc, Aspirin, and Quercetin. The FLCCC just added Fluvoxamine to their early outpatient treatment cocktail.

Whatever you do, unless you are using Ivermectin for prophylaxis, never forget that multi-drug cocktail treatment is the best strategy for COVID-19.

Unfortunately, vaccines against rapidly mutating RNA viruses have a major weakness, and that is that resistance against them rapidly develops. We already see this with the Indian variant, the Brazilian, and the South African strain. So the answer is not more boosters.

Beyond this, the current vaccines are fraught with a toxic protein, the spike protein. This spicule is itself inherently harmful even in the absence of virus, and it can produce long-term symptoms – similar in most ways to COVID-19. Fortunately, Ivermectin binds to this toxic spike and can help neutralize its activity through binding inhibition.

This is why Dr. Paul Marik is developing a treatment protocol for Long Hauler's syndrome centered around Ivermectin. It is called the I-RECOVER protocol. Dr. Marik's team is also developing the I-MASS protocol for the world – an Ivermectin-based strategy to prevent and treat large populations. It will soon be unveiled on FLCCC.net

Dr. Peter McCullough's warning about the dangers of the spike protein contained in the mRNA vaccine should not be taken lightly. He and I are not anti-vaxxers. We are both for safe and properly tested vaccines, but this one is different. It is experimental, and it is riddled with an unacceptable number of adverse events and deaths.

Dr. McCullough, among the most published cardiologists in the world, and an epidemiologist said this about the COVID-19 vaccine,

"This is far and away the most lethal, toxic, biologic agent ever injected into a human body in America history, and its going strong, with no mention of safety by our officials, with wild enthusiasm by our hospitals and hospital administrators, with doctors supporting it..." See the 1:37.08 mark in this video where he reports this.

https://vimeo.com/553518199

Post-Script: Cancer & Viruses

As a medical professional, I have always recommended vaccines before this. But, currently, I cannot recommend anyone else get the vaccine when we have effective anti-viral therapy like Ivermectin and the rest of the cocktails.

Let me leave you all with the hope that the Pandemic will soon be brought to a conclusion, as the world adopts Ivermectin and sequential multi-drug therapy as the standard of care.

https://www.amjmed.com/article/S0002-9343(20)30673-2/fulltext

As we all get back to work, and as we all begin to enjoy a normal life again, allow me to ask you to help me get the word out on Repurposed Drug Cocktails for terminal cancer – in addition to the standard of care. Almost 1.9 million Americans are diagnosed with cancer each year, and over 600 thousand die from the disease.

My research shows that by adding repurposed drug cocktails, we can drop both of these numbers by 1/3. Think of dropping new cases by 600 thousand and having 200 thousand fewer deaths. Of course, now you know why Big Pharma will never agree to this as billions of dollars in treatment costs will also be saved.

After this COVID-19 debacle with Big Pharma, please do not believe that repurposed drug cocktails are trivial. They worked for COVID – better than Big Pharma's more expensive solution, and I know they are also effective in treating most terminal cancer patients.

The first step in adding a repurposed drug cocktail is to call the Care Oncology Clinic for anyone with terminal cancer. They have branches now in the United States or the United Kingdom. 1-800-392-1353.

https://careoncology.com/

Justus R. Hope, MD

Redding, California

June 6, 2021

TITLES BY HOPE PRESSWORKS INTERNATIONAL, LLC

www.HopePressworks.org

CHRONIC PAIN

- How to End Your Back Pain Nightmare, 1st Edition
- How to End Your Back Pain Nightmare, 25th Anniversary Edition

THE OPIOID EPIDEMIC

- The Physician Primer, Prescribe Like a Lawyer
- The Physician Primer 2.0, The Safe Opioid Protocol

THE OBESITY EPIDEMIC

- The Coffee Cure Diet

CANCER

- Surviving Cancer, COVID-19, and Disease: The Repurposed Drug Revolution

HUMAN RIGHTS

- Ivermectin for the World

ABOUT THE AUTHOR

Dr. Justus Robert Hope, writer's pseudonym, graduated summa cum laude from Wabash College where he was named a Lilly Scholar. He attended Baylor College of Medicine, where he was awarded the M.D. degree. He completed a residency in Physical Medicine & Rehabilitation at The University of California Irvine Medical Center.

He is board certified and has taught at the University of California Davis Medical Center in the departments of Family Practice and Physical Medicine & Rehabilitation. He has practiced medicine for over 35 years and maintains a private practice in Northern California. He has authored six books.